*Chemical Warfare in World War I:
The American Experience, 1917-1918*

Chemical Warfare in World War I: The American Experience, 1917-1918

by MAJ(P) Charles E. Heller, USAR

University Press of the Pacific
Honolulu, Hawaii

Chemical Warfare in World War I:
The American Experience, 1917-1918

by
Charles E. Heller

ISBN: 1-4102-2261-6

Copyright © 2005 by University Press of the Pacific

Reprinted from the 1984 edition

University Press of the Pacific
Honolulu, Hawaii
http://www.universitypressofthepacific.com

FOREWORD

This Book chronicles the introduction of chemical agents in World War I, the U.S. Army's tentative preparations for gas warfare prior to and after American entry into the war, and the AEF experience with gas on the Western Front.

Chemical warfare affected tactics and almost changed the outcome of World War I. The overwhelming success of the first use of gas caught both sides by surprise. Fortunately, the pace of hostilities permitted the Allies to develop a suitable defense to German gas attacks and eventually to field a considerable offensive chemical capability. Nonetheless, from the introduction of chemical warfare in early 1915 until Armistice Day in November, 1918, the Allies were usually one step behind their German counterparts in the development of gas doctrine and the employment of gas tactics and procedures.

In his final report to Congress on World War I, General John J. Pershing expressed the sentiment of contemporary senior officers when he said, "Whether or not gas will be employed in future wars is a matter of conjecture, but the effect is so deadly to the unprepared that we can never afford to neglect the question." General Pershing was the last American field commander actually to confront chemical agents on the battlefield. Today, in light of a significant Soviet chemical threat and solid evidence of chemical warfare in Southeast and Southwest Asia, it is by no means certain he will retain that distinction.

Over 50 percent of the Total Army's Chemical Corps assets are located within the United States Army Reserve. This Book was prepared by the USAR Staff Officer serving with the Combat Studies Institute, USACGSC, after a number of requests from USAR Chemical Corps officers for a historical study on the nature of chemical warfare in World War I. In fulfilling the needs of the USAR, this book also meets the needs of the Total Army in its preparations to fight, if necessary, on a battlefield where chemical agents might be employed.

CARL E. VUONO
Lieutenant General, USA
Commandant

Contents

Contents

Illustrations

Maps

Figures

Tables

Introduction

The combat experience of World War I provided the U.S. Army with its first significant exposure to chemical warfare. The purpose of this paper is to show how the Army prepared for this kind of warfare and how soldiers in the American Expeditionary Forces (AEF), from generals to doughboys, adapted or failed to adapt to fighting a war in which chemical weapons played a prominent role. Because no one AEF division experienced every facet of gas warfare, the study will examine information pertaining to many units in order to give a more complete picture of the phenomenon.

In World War I terms, chemical warfare included not only gas, but liquid flammable material, thermite, and smoke (all of which are relevant to the modern battlefield). This study will deal only with what participants referred to as "chemicals," "gases," or "war gases." These included real gases such as phosgene and chlorine, and also weapons that, while referred to as gases, were in fact vaporized liquids (mustard gas, for example) or finely ground solids. In this study the terms "chemical agent" and "gas" will be used interchangeably. Smoke will be discussed, but only as a *ruse de guerre* for gas; liquid flame and thermite will not be covered. Because most of the U.S. experience was on the Western Front, that theater of the war will receive detailed treatment.

Despite technological advances in chemical warfare since 1918, many lessons learned on the battlefields of World War I are valid for study today, if only because America's principal antagonist in world affairs, the Soviet Union, appears to be quite willing to employ chemical agents on today's battlefield. During the decade of the 1970s persistent accounts of the use of chemical agents by the Russians and their clients caused the U.S. government to pay closer attention to the problem of chemical warfare. Soviet offensive equipment captured by the Israelis in the 1973 October War contained filtration systems for survival on a chemical or biological battlefield. Reports from Laos about Vietnamese using a chemical agent called "Yellow Rain" on mountain tribesmen prompted a policy review by U.S. government officials. In December, 1979, the Soviet invasion of Afghanistan, with subsequent reports from Afghan refugees that the invaders were using gas during combat operations, again forced the U.S. Army to reassess its chemical warfare doctrine.[1]

U.S. intelligence estimates indicate that the Russians have between 70,000 and 100,000 chemical warfare troops. Every Soviet line regiment has a Chemical Defense Company. Present Soviet chemical delivery systems include artillery, mortars, multiple rocket launchers, bombs, air spray, and land mines. The blood, blister, and nerve agents in the Russian chemical arsenal include mustard gas (a blister agent) and phosgene (a lung injurant)—two of the most effective agents used in World War I.[2]

There is an abundance of material available for a study of gas warfare during World War I. Sources include unit reports, the published and unpublished diaries of participants, books written by chemical officers during the interwar period, and a number of secondary historical works of more recent origin. Also, I conducted several interviews with veterans of the First World War to obtain as accurate a picture as possible of what it was like for an AEF doughboy to train for, and to live, work, and fight in, a chemical environment. During the war the newly created Chemical Warfare Service (CWS)* did its best to record its activities and report on the use of chemicals. I relied extensively on these records.

A number of agencies provided a great deal of assistance to me in the preparation of this paper, and I would like to acknowledge the staffs of the following institutions: the Technical Library, Chemical Systems Laboratory, Edgewood Area, Aberdeen Proving Ground; U.S. Army Chemical Center and School, Fort McClellan, Alabama; National Archives, Washington, D.C.; Military History Institute, Carlisle Barracks, Pennsylvania; and Combined Arms Research Library, U.S. Army Command and General Staff College, Fort Leavenworth, Kansas. I especially want to thank members of the 1st Gas Regiment Association for graciously consenting to be interviewed, and Lt. Col. Charles M. Wurm, Chemical Corps, CACDA, Fort Leavenworth, for providing me with a great amount of technical information and advice.

Major(P) Charles Heller, USAR
Combat Studies Institute
U.S. Army Command and General Staff College

*The forerunner of the CWS was the Gas Service, set up under AEF General Order 31, 3 September 1917. On 11 May 1918, when the CWS was established as a branch of the National Army, the Gas Service became the Overseas Division, CWS.

The Introduction of Gas Warfare in World War I

Of all the weapons employed in World War I, none stimulated public revulsion more than poison gas. The abhorrence of chemical warfare lingered long after the Armistice of 11 November 1918. Gas victims continually reminded the general public of the effect of chemical weapons, as illustrated by the often repeated story of a veteran's coughing fit being explained by a tap on the chest and an apologetic, "Gas you know."

The employment of chemical agents in war, however, did not begin with World War I. The earliest recorded incident occurred in the fifth century B.C. during one of a series of wars between Athens and Sparta.*[1] Over the centuries that followed, combatants on several occasions engaged in rudimentary forms of chemical warfare on the battlefield. If by the end of the nineteenth century the use of poison gas was still by far the exception and not the rule in war, there were in all the great powers a number of men who foresaw its widespread use should a general conflagration engulf Europe.[2]

A concern with poison gas manifested itself at the Hague Conference of 1899. One of the agenda items dealt with prohibiting the use of shells filled with asphyxiating gas. The proposed ban** eventually passed with one dissenting vote, that of the American representative, Naval Capt. Alfred T. Mahan, who declared that "it was illogical and not demonstrably humane to be tender about asphyxiating men with gas, when all were prepared to admit that it was allowable to blow the bottom out of an ironclad at midnight, throwing four or five hundred men into the sea, to be choked by water, with scarcely the remotest chance of escape." Secretary of State John Hay, in his instructions to Mahan, argued that the inventiveness of Americans should not be restricted in the development of new weapons. For Hay it made no sense for the United States to deprive itself of the ability to use, at some later date, a weapon that might prove to be more humane and effective than anything then present in the American arsenal.[3]

---

*Spartan forces besieging an Athenian city placed a lighted mixture of wood, pitch, and sulfur under the walls. The Spartans hoped the fumes would incapacitate the Athenians so that they would not be able to resist the assault that followed.

**The declaration stated, "The Contracting Powers agree to abstain from the use of projectiles the sole object of which is the diffusion of asphyxiating or deleterious gasses."

The Hague Conference declaration did not prevent some nations from discussing the use of chemical weapons, and at least one country, France, experimented publicly with gas. The French Army tested a grenade filled with ethyl bromoacetate, a nontoxic tear, or lachrymatory, agent developed for use in the suppression of small-arms fire from the concrete casements then prevalent in the permanent fortifications that dotted Western Europe. In 1912, French police used 26-mm grenades filled with this agent to capture a notorious gang of Parisian bank robbers. The Germans, unlike the French, did not experiment with chemical agents for military use as such, but at the outbreak of World War I, Germany's highly advanced dye industry gave it a sophisticated technological base from which to develop weapons of this nature.[4]

When war erupted in August, 1914, everyone from private citizens to the leaders of the belligerent countries shared a common belief that the economies of the European nations would neither survive nor support a lengthy war. As a result, the war plans of two key protagonists, Germany and France, called for a quick, decisive offensive against one another. Kaiser Wilhelm II of Germany assured his troops that they would be "home before the leaves fall." It was not to be. By the end of 1914, the armies on the Western Front were locked in a deadly form of trench warfare (Map 1),* sustained by the very industrialized economies that, because of their complexity and interdependency, had been thought unable to withstand a long war.[5]

Unwilling to accept the indecisiveness of trench warfare, army staffs on both sides pondered ways to break the deadlock and return to open or maneuver warfare. Alternatives were proposed, some strategic, others tactical. The British, for example, sought a strategic solution by a seaborne assault against Turkey, an ally of Germany. This attack at Gallipoli in 1915 sought to open the Dardanelles as the first step toward linking up with Russia and forcing Turkey out of the war. For a variety of reasons, the plan failed, and the deadlock on the Western Front continued.

As their attack at Gallipoli tottered to defeat, the British looked to the application of tactical innovation at Neuve-Chapelle to break the stalemate. On 10 March 1915 British artillery, instead of firing a lengthy bombardment prior to an attack, as doctrine dictated, let loose a brief but intense barrage on a relatively narrow German trench frontage. The fire was then shifted to the German rear in order to create a lethal steel curtain that would block reinforcements. To the surprise of everyone, the British infantry quickly

*One of the misconceptions surrounding World War I is that there existed a continuous, parallel belt of trenches stretching from the English Channel in the north to the Swiss border in the south. In fact, in some sectors along the 470-mile Western Front, soldiers occupied shell holes; in other areas, the terrain caused troops to be dispersed in fortified garrisons or strong points. Some trenches, as in the British sector of Flanders, were actually sandbagged parapets rising from marshy lands, where digging any deeper than a foot or two would have brought water to the surface. There was one factor, however, that was constant along the entire front. Whether in trenches, shell holes, or strong points, daily life offered little more than dull routine and boredom for the men of both sides as they waited for their respective high commands to decide their fate.

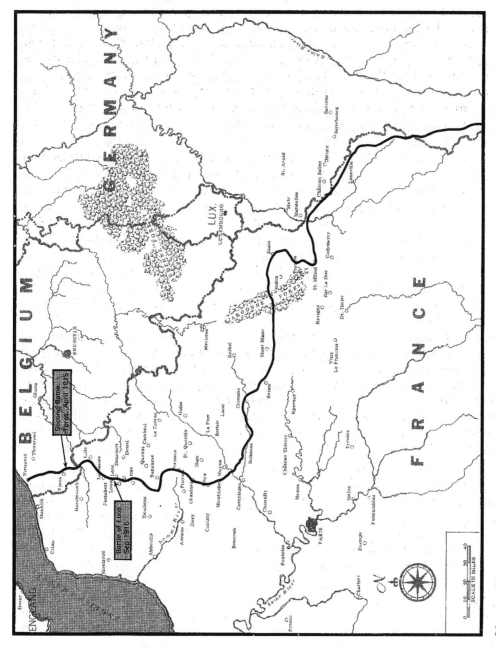

Map 1. The stabilized Western Front, 1915.

overran the German forward positions. The attack failed, though, primarily because the high command, viewing it as an experiment, did not have sufficient reserves available to exploit a breakthrough.

Germany also searched for ways to break the deadlock and decided on a solution involving gas. Early in the war the Germans kept a wary eye out for indications that the French were using their 26-mm gas grenades. Apparently, in August, 1914, France did use this chemical weapon, but in open areas where the gas quickly dispersed with no noticeable effect on the enemy. The French soon discarded the grenades as worthless. At this same time, stories were appearing in Allied newspapers about a new French liquid explosive, turpinite. While claiming that this substance gave off lethal fumes, the articles failed to explain that the gas reached a deadly concentration only in confined spaces. Still, the Germans were apprehensive and became alarmed by the deaths of a number of soldiers asphyxiated during a French bombardment, even though a medical team rushed to the scene concluded that the men died not from poison gas, but from inhaling carbon monoxide fumes while huddled in their dugout.[6]

In any event such newspaper stories and front-line experiences may have spurred the development of war gases by German scientists. Contributing to that effort, chemistry professor Walter Nernst suggested partially replacing the TNT in a 105-mm shrapnel shell with dianisidine chlorosulphonate, an agent known to cause irritation of the mucous membrane. The new filling would serve two purposes: it would conserve TNT and act as a chemical weapon. The German High Command accepted this new weapon, although it is uncertain which of the two purposes it initially considered more important. On 27 October 1914, 3,000 of these shells fell on British troops near Neuve-Chapelle. The soldiers suffered no ill effects and never suspected they were under chemical attack. The Germans continued to experiment with gas because they were convinced the idea had merit and because intelligence sources could not determine what effect the shells had had at Neuve-Chapelle. This lack of information on the effects of gas attacks was a common occurrence throughout the war.[7]

The Neuve-Chapelle experiment increased the German High Command's interest in gas warfare. The German General Staff asked the Kaiser Wilhelm Institute for Physical Chemistry and Electrochemistry in Berlin to investigate the possibility of using a more effective agent. The only guideline provided by the military was that the Hague declaration of 1899, banning projectiles used exclusively for delivering poison gases, had to be circumvented. Adhering to the letter if not the spirit of the ban, the Germans devised a gas shell that also contained an explosive charge for producing a shrapnel effect. The Professor von Tappan who designed the shell also solved two technical problems related to emplacing chemicals in an artillery projectile. First, he stabilized the liquid within a shell casing in order to reduce its tumbling in flight, thereby increasing the shell's accuracy and range. Second, to ensure that two extremely reactive chemical substances did not accidently combine in the shell casing, von Tappan developed a special shell, designated the T-shell by the German Army in his honor. The T-shell was a standard

15-cm howitzer round that contained seven pounds of xylyl bromide and a burster charge for a splinter effect. A lead lining prevented contact between the burster charge and the chemical payload.[8]

The German High Command decided to use the first T-shells on the Eastern Front. On 31 January 1915, over 18,000 shells were fired at Russian positions at Bolimov. German officers, confident that their new weapon would neutralize the enemy positions, were surprised when their attack was repulsed with severe casualties. The shelling had had little or no effect on the Russians because cold temperatures had prevented vaporization of the xylyl bromide.[9]

To find a more effective means of employing gas on the battlefield, the German High Command turned to an assistant of von Tappan, Professor Fritz Haber. Haber, a reservist, had shown marked enthusiasm for the potential value of chemicals as weapons. Believing that T-shells did not provide a high enough concentration of chemicals to produce enemy casualties, he suggested the use of large commercial gas cylinders as a delivery system. Cylinders could deliver large amounts of gas and, like the T-shell, did not technically violate the Hague ban on projectiles. Haber also recommended the use of chlorine as an agent because it was commercially produced and readily available in large quantities. Chlorine also satisfied the requirements for military application: it was lethal, immediately effective, nonpersistent, and volatile. It was also dense enough to resist dilution in a moderate wind.[10]

Haber's gas cylinder project received the approval of the Chief of the German General Staff, General Erich von Falkenhayn, who had the professor appointed Head of the Chemical Warfare Department in the Prussian Ministry of War. The high command selected the front of the Fourth Army facing the French salient at Ypres as the location for an experimental attack. Pioneer Regiment 35 was designated to conduct the gas attack. Haber, assigned as a "chemico-technical advisor," assisted Colonel Peterson, the regimental commander, and instructed the troops on the emplacement and use of gas cylinders. By 10 March 1915 the Regiment, with the assistance of infantry labor, had emplaced 1,600 large and 4,130 small cylinders containing a total of 168 tons of chlorine. Then, for one month, the Pioneer troops sat and waited for the winds to shift westerly toward the enemy trenches in the Ypres salient. Only then could they safely unleash the chemicals by opening the cylinder valves.[11]

Late in the afternoon of 22 April 1915, a setting sun cast long shadows over the battle-scarred terrain around the medieval Belgium city of Ypres. In the distance the faint sound of large-caliber guns could be heard. Birds fluttered and swooped, seeking places to roost on the practically treeless landscape. Suddenly, at 1724, three flares rose from an observation balloon over the German lines and burst against the darkening eastern sky. German artillery commenced a fierce bombardment that landed to the rear of the French and British lines in the Ypres sector. Then, at 1800, an eerie silence fell over the area.

German Pioneer troops opening cylinders for a gas attack, 1916.

Peering across the battlefield, men of two French divisions, the 87th Territorial and the 45th Algerian, saw blue-white wisps of haze rising from the German trenches. The haze swirled about, gathered in a cloud that slowly turned yellow-green, and began to drift across the terrain at a height of up to six feet. As the cloud drifted, it settled into every depression in the landscape. Finally, the gentle north-northeasterly wind brought it spilling into the French trenches, silently enveloping the occupants in a misty, deadly embrace.

To the north and southwest of the now mist-enshrouded French positions, British and Canadian troops looked into the haze and, to their amazement, saw soldiers, many without weapons, emerge from the cloud, "running wildly and in confusion" toward positions to the rear. Terror-stricken Algerians ran by the startled Dominion troops, coughing and clutching their throats. Moments later French soldiers staggered by, "blinded, coughing, chests heaving, faces an ugly purple color, lips speechless with agony." One by one, the guns of the French artillery batteries in the sector stopped firing, and the two French divisions collapsed. The Ypres front now had a gap over four-miles wide containing hundreds of men in a "comatose or dying condition." After half an hour, German troops, equipped with cotton wadding tied over their faces—a primitive form of protective mask—cautiously advanced into the breech created by the discharge of chlorine gas.

Following the initial shock and surprise, Allied commanders began to bring forward reserve troops and to move units from the left and right flank into the gap. The Germans advanced four and one-half miles until they encountered the ragged edge of a hurriedly organized defensive line (Map 2). The First Canadian Division and assorted French troops manned

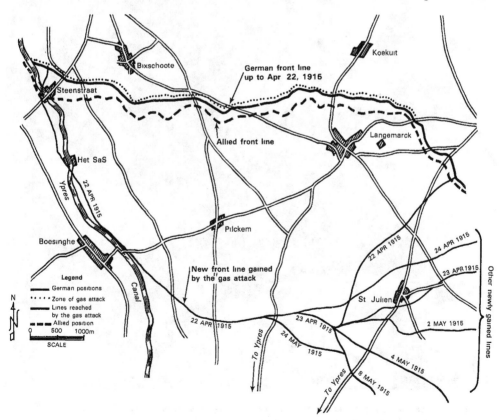

Map 2. Ypres sector in Belgium, 22 April—24 May 1915.

the line in scattered, hastily prepared positions 1,000 to 3,000 yards apart. This improvised defense, together with the fact that the Germans had lost some of their combat edge during the month-long wait for favorable winds, finally slowed and then halted the attack. As for the German troops who reached their initial objective, they had only the most primitive protective equipment. When they saw the havoc their own gas had wrought, they had no wish to proceed any farther that night.

Two days later, during which time the British and French brought reinforcements into the area, the Germans discharged more gas. Although they did so again four more times throughout May, the element of surprise had been lost. The British and French troops were now equipped with their own primitive masks, and although the defenders suffered severe losses (over 5,900 casualties—nearly double the number of casualties for the attackers), the Germans could gain no more than a few hundred yards beyond the forward limit of their first attack. The German High Command, surprised as its opponents at the success of the new weapon, had no reserves to exploit a possible success. Thus, one of the war's greatest tactical surprises was dissipated on what amounted to an experimental attack with limited objectives.[12]

German medics, wearing an early mask, giving oxygen to gas victim, 1915. British, French, and Russian prototype masks were similar in design.

With the battle front at Ypres now stabilized, the British and French had to decide whether or not to retaliate in kind. Faced with the Germans' obvious technological advantage, the Allies at first hesitated to retaliate for fear of inviting the expansion of gas warfare. But when the British Expeditionary Force commander reported that a lack of an offensive gas capability would seriously impair the morale of his troops, the British cabinet gave its approval to use chemical agents. The French government soon followed suit for basically the same reason.[13]

On 24 September 1915, at 0550 near Loos, Belgium, the British launched the Allies' first attack supported by gas. It had taken them five frantic months to reach a point at which a large-scale gas attack was feasible. During that period, several "Special Companies" of Royal Engineers had been trained in the emplacement and discharge of gas cylinders. Unlike the Germans, the British decided to conduct their gas attack on a wide frontage. This necessitated the deployment of the cylinders clustered in batteries along the front rather than spaced far apart in one continuous line. To accomplish this, the British constructed galleries in front of the first-line trenches and positioned in them 5,500 cylinders containing 150 tons of chlorine.* The frontage was too wide to saturate all of it with gas, so the British decided to utilize smoke candles to simulate gas in those areas where the agent could not be used. By alternating the discharges of gas and smoke, the gas attack could be prolonged over forty minutes. This planned smoke screen was the first used during the war.

Fortune did not favor this first British gas attack. During the evening prior to the attack, the winds died. The following morning the British commander, Gen. Sir Douglas Haig, made a controversial decision to proceed with the attack despite uncertainty as to whether or not the slight breeze that rose in the morning would continue to blow toward the German lines. On the right flank, the gentle winds brought the gas and smoke mixture into the German trench system. There, the mild wind worked to the British advantage, for the cloud lingered and did not dissipate. On the left flank, however, not only did the winds fail, but in several positions the gas wafted back into the British trenches, engulfing the troops waiting to attack.

The Germans were taken by surprise. Their troops had little awareness of the danger posed by gas and were not sufficiently trained in defensive measures. The war diary of the German Sixth Army, the unit that bore the brunt of the attack, described the results. The gas in some instances caused little but momentary confusion, while in other cases entire units lost their ability to resist the follow-up British infantry attack. The German mask, which was essentially the same one used at Ypres, broke down as the gas lingered. The chlorine also caused rifles, machine guns, and even artillery breechblocks to jam. The most effective result of the gas was that it rendered German officers and noncommissioned officers (NCOs) incapable of shouting commands loud enough to be heard through their masks. The dense clouds

---

*This forward placement was made to protect the cylinders from German artillery, which was zeroed in on the first line of trenches to the rear of the galleries.

of smoke and gas also shrouded positions and precluded officers and NCOs from leading by example.[14]

In spite of some British gains, the attack fell short of the desired results for three reasons. The first was the decision to proceed with the attack despite the unfavorable wind conditions. Second, the British artillery was hampered in providing support because it lacked sufficient shells. Third, there were no reserve divisions to exploit a breakthrough. In his report, the British Commander-in-Chief, Sir John French, acknowledged that, although the attack failed to penetrate the German lines, the "gas attack met with marked success, and produced a demoralizing effect in some of its opposing units." More important, the major belligerents had accepted and expanded the use of chemicals as weapons of war.[15]

The ensuing chemical war proved to be one of experimentation with gases and with defensive and offensive equipment. As tactical doctrine and training evolved to reflect technological changes, the availability of gases and the imagination of commanders became the only limits to the employment of this new weapon.

The Europeans Face Chemicals on the Battlefield, 1915-1918

2

During World War I chemists on both sides investigated over 3,000 chemical substances for potential use as weapons. Of these, only thirty agents were used in combat, and only about a dozen achieved the desired military results (Table 1). Most armies grouped war gases according to their physiological effects, that is their effects on the human body.[1]

One category, lachrymators, was composed of tear gases such as xylyl bromide, an agent that primarily affected the eyes but in large concentrations could also damage the respiratory system. Asphyxiators, such as phosgene, chloropicrin, and chlorine, were in another category. These gases caused fluid to enter the lungs, thereby preventing oxygen from reaching the blood. Toxic gases, yet another category, passed through the lungs to the blood, preventing the circulation and release of oxygen throughout the body. Hydrogen cyanide ("Vincennite" to the French) was one of the least effective toxic agents. Sternutators, such as diphenylchlorarsine, were a type of respiratory irritant composed of a very fine dust that caused sneezing, nausea, and vomiting. Some sternutators were systemic poisons that had a delayed toxic effect on the body. The final category held the greatest casualty producer—a vesicant or blister agent that, because of its peculiar odor, the British and later the Americans commonly referred to as "mustard gas."*[2]

In 1917 the Germans first used mustard against the Allies at Ypres. This was the only persistent agent used during World War I and had effects similar to those produced by a combination of lachrymatory, asphyxiator, and systemic poisons. Although called mustard *gas*, this chemical was not a gas, but rather a volatile liquid that, several hours after contact with the skin, would cause severe burns and blisters. The introduction of Yellow Cross caught the Allies completely by surprise. During the first attack, British infantry saw the gas shells explode, but were unable to "see, smell or taste any agent, nor feel any immediate effects." The soldiers concluded that the Germans were trying to trick them and did not put on their masks. After several hours, to the consternation of officers and medics, the troops began to complain of pain in their eyes, throats, and lungs. Later, blisters appeared on the exposed skin of the British soldiers. The German use of Yellow Cross

*The Germans referred to it as "Yellow Cross" because of the shell marking, and the French called it "Yperite," in recognition of the location where it was first used.

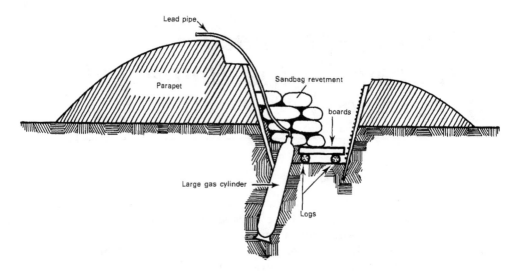

Figure 1. Side view of gas cylinder emplacement.

caused British gas casualties, which had been declining, to increase markedly. Because of its ability to produce large numbers of casualties, mustard was soon being referred to as the "King" of the war gases.[3]

The major combatants realized that the employment of gas called for specially trained troops and, accordingly, formed offensive gas units. Because of the need to emplace gas cylinders, pioneer or engineer troops usually provided the cadre of these special units. The Germans converted two pioneer regiments, the 35th and 36th, into gas units consisting of three battalions each. The regiments would deploy by companies, according to the size of the front of the attack. In addition to these units, the Germans organized a gas mortar (*Minenwerfen*) battalion. The Austro-Hungarians followed the German model and created their own special gas units.[4]

As early as July, 1915, the French and British organized gas companies called "Special" by the British and "Z" for *gaz* (gas) by the French; both employed engineer troops as cadre. By 1917 the British had expanded their original four companies to twenty-one and had organized them as a Special Brigade. The French eventually created the 31st, 32nd, and 33rd gas battalions composed of three companies each. The Russians organized gas units and called them "Gas Detachments of the Chemical Department," with one detachment assigned to each Russian Army, a total of thirteen.[5]

In addition to developing gas units and chemical agents, a constant search continued for efficient delivery systems. The cylinders used in the first gas attack at Ypres in 1915 were the major component of a cumbersome, immobile system. It usually took several days of intensive labor,* with infantry providing most of the muscle, to emplace the cylinders for a cloud attack (Figure 1). One can gain an indication of the difficulty of the task by noting that as many as 12,000 cylinders, each weighing over 100 pounds,

*The time it took to install individual cylinders varied according to the terrain, weather, available manpower, and enemy harassing fire.

French Number	Shell Filling	American and British Code Symbols	French Designation	German Designation and Shell Marking	Odor	Persistency		Physiological Effect	Remarks
						In Open	In Woods		
				Non-Persistent Class.					
	Chlorine (Used only in cloud gas)	Red Star	Bertholite		Chloride of Lime	10 min.	3 hrs.	Lung Irritant, Deadly. Action Immediate.	These gases are very volatile; they are vaporized entirely at the moment of explosion, forming a cloud capable of giving deadly effects, but which loses more or less rapidly its effectiveness by dilution and dispersion into the atmosphere.
4	Arsenic Trichloride 30% / Stannic Chloride 15% / Hydrogen Cyanide 50% / Chloroform 5%	Not used by A.E.F. or B.E.F.	Vincennite			10 min	3 hrs	Lachrymator and Respiratory Irritant. Considered quite toxic, but in high concentrations only.	
4B	Cyanogen Chloride 70% / Arsenic Trichloride 30%		Vitrite			10 min.	3 hrs.	A Lachrymator, Respiratory Irritant and Lethal Agent	
5	Diphenyl Chlorarsine	D.A	Sternite	Blue Cross	Slight	10 min.	3 hrs.	Sneezing Gas. Nerve Depressant. Respiratory Irritant.	These gases form non-persistant clouds of solid particles.
	Diphenyl Cyanarsine	D.C	Sternite	Blue Cross	Is interchangeable with D.A			Effects somewhat greater.	
	Phosgene	C.G	Collongite	Three White bands. White D.	Musty Hay, Green Corn	10 min.	3 hrs.	Respiratory Irritant. Very deadly. Action usually slightly delayed.	
				Semi-Persistent Class.					
	Diphosgene	Not used in S.F.	Superpalite	Green Cross	Disagreeable, suffocating. Musty Hay	3 hrs.	12 hrs.	Same as phosgene.	These gases have moderately high boiling points, are only partially vaporized at the moment of explosion. The cloud formed upon explosion is generally not deadly, but it immediately gives penetrative lacrymatory or irritant effects. The majority of the "gas" contents of the shell is pulverized and projected in the form of a spray or fog which slowly settles on the ground and continues to give off vapors which prolong the action of the initial cloud.
	Phenyl Carbylamine Chloride			Green Cross		3 hrs.	12 hrs.	Eye, Nose and Throat Irritant. Not very poisonous.	
	Phosgene, Diphosgene and Diphenyl Chlorazine			Green Cross 2	Resembles Diphosgene a little pungent	3 hrs.	12 hrs.	Respiratory Irritant. Slightly delayed action. Very deadly. Causes vomiting and a little lachrymation.	
	Chlorpicrin 75% / Phosgene 25%	P.G.			Pungent, Suffocating.	3 hrs.	12 hrs.	Causes vomiting. Respiratory Irritant, a little lachrymation.	

NOTE: The above figures on time of persistency are approximate only and for calm weather. Persistency is dependent to a large extent on temperature, wind velocity, and the amount of gas liberated, especially in woods or other more or less closed places. High temperatures and wind velocities decrease persistency, and low temperatures and wind velocities increase it.

Table 1. Summary of markings for chemical shell and properties of most common gases.

French Number	Shell Filling	American and British Code Symbols	French Designation	German Designation and Shell Marking	Odor	Persistency In Open	Persistency In Woods	Physiological Effect	Remarks
						Semi-Persistent Class.			
	Diphosgene and Chlorpicrin			Green Cross 1	Pungent, Suffocating	3 hrs.	12 hrs.	Slightly delayed action, very deadly, respiratory irritant, causes vomiting and a little lachrymation.	Phosgene in these mixtures has same effect as used above, if concentration is sufficiently high.
7	Chlorpicrin	P.S.	Aquinite		Pungent	3 hrs.	12 hrs.	Causes vomiting, respiratory irritant, tear producer.	
	Chlorpicrin 80% Stannic Chloride 20%	N.C.			Pungent	3 hrs.	12 hrs.	Respiratory irritant, causes vomiting, tear producer.	
	Ethyl Dichlorarsine and Dichlormethylether			Yellow Cross 1 or Green Cross 3	Ethereal; Pleasant	3 hrs.	12 hrs.	Nerve poison similar to diphenylchlorarsine, easily destroyed by water.	
						Persistent Class.			
9	Bromacetone	B.A.	Martonite			2 days	7 days	Lachrymator, Tear Producer.	These gases having very high boiling points are but little vaporized at the moment of explosion. A small portion of the contents of the shell is atomized and gives immediate effect, but by far the greater part is projected on the ground in the form of droplets which slowly vaporize and continue the action of the initial cloud.
	Brom Ketones			Green Cross	Pungent	3 days	7 days	Tear Producers, Slight Respiratory Irritants. Action immediate.	
21	Brombenzylcyanide	C.A.	Camite		No Odor	3 days	7 days	Not toxic but most powerful lachrymator known.	
20	Mustard Gas (Dichlorethyl Sulphide)	H.S.	Yperite	Yellow Cross	Slight Mustard or Garlic	3 days	7 days	Respiratory Irritant. Eye and Skin Irritant. Blistering Agent. Action delayed several hours.	

NOTE: The above figures on time of persistency are approximate only and for calm weather. Persistency is dependent to a large extent on temperature, wind velocity, and the amount of gas liberated, especially in woods or other more or less closed places. High temperatures and wind velocities decrease persistency, and low temperatures and wind velocities increase it.

Table 1. Summary of markings for chemical shell and properties of most common gases. —Continued

were sometimes needed for a single operation. Once emplaced, the cylinders were dangerously exposed to enemy high explosive shells and easily damaged. Cylinder discharges always depended on favorable weather conditions.

Despite these problems, the British relied on cylinders as a delivery method until the end of the war. They normally used seven to eight cylinders in a section, six sections to a Special Brigade company. Sixteen companies could produce a gas wave or cloud that covered a 24,000-meter front. Several factors influenced the British decision to continue using cylinders. First, the prevailing winds favored Allied gas clouds. Second, the British suffered from a chronic shortage of shells and were reluctant to convert the production of high explosive shells to the production of gas shells. Third, British intelligence reports indicated a dense cloud attack was effective in producing mass casualties. On 26 October 1917, Brig. Gen. Charles H. Foulkes, Commander of the British Special Brigade, reviewed intelligence reports indicating that British cloud attacks created significant German casualties as far back as thirty kilometers from the front-line trenches. Foulkes proposed that the Special Brigade use what he termed "retired cylinder attacks," in which a large number of cylinders would be emplaced *behind* British lines rather than in the front lines or forward of the trenches. Because the Special Brigade companies could assemble a greater number of cylinders in a relatively small area without the interference of enemy small arms or shell fire, this method allowed for a significantly greater concentration of gas released at one point.[6]

The British improved this tactic by conducting what they called "beam attacks." These attacks called for placing numerous cylinders on narrow-gauge tram cars that troops pushed forward to positions just behind the front trenches. After the cylinders were opened, the resulting gas concentration became so dense that friendly troops had to be evacuated from the path of the gas "beam." On 24 May 1918 the British launched their first beam attack. This and similiar attacks, General Foulkes claimed, caused the Germans considerable anxiety, for they could not determine how and where the dense clouds originated. The beam attacks were especially deadly when launched from six or more separate railheads and when the individual clouds merged behind German lines. Prisoners taken from the German 9th Uhlan Regiment reported that one such attack caused 500 casualties in the neighboring 1st Landwehr Regiment, which, as a result of the attack, had to be withdrawn from the line. According to the British, the effectiveness of the improved cloud attacks, with their increased density, continued to frustrate the German Army.[7]

The Germans, for their part, arranged their cylinders so that twenty formed a battery. Fifty such batteries were required to saturate one kilometer of front line with gas. The lack of favorable prevailing winds, however, soon forced the Germans to abandon the cloud attack. On 8 August 1916, they launched their last cylinder attack at Wieltje, near the scene of the first discharge at Ypres.[8]

Narrow gauge tram gondola with gas cylinders

Because the prevailing winds in Western Europe blew from west to east, the German Army began to place increasing reliance on gas-filled shells that detonated beyond Allied lines and whose contents could then drift back over enemy trenches. Gas shells could be fired from standard artillery pieces with no extensive adaptation for gas employment. Although weather conditions still remained a factor, no longer did the Germans have to wait for the wind to change to a westerly direction. Now artillery could fire upward of the target, saturating it with gas and achieving the same effect as cylinders. Shells also offered an element of surprise not available with cloud attacks. Finally, gas shells proved more advantageous than high explosive rounds because the former did not have to score direct hits on a target to neutralize it. To avoid confusion and to aid artillerymen, the Germans developed a coded system of colored crosses to identify shells containing chemical agents.

The Germans were further encouraged to use gas shells by the results of an attack staged on the night of 22—23 June 1916. About 110,000 shells containing the lung irritant Green Cross fell on French forces near the fortress of Verdun. German batteries adjacent to this sector added thousands of rounds of a lachrymatory gas. The gas attack, according to French sources, had its greatest effect on French artillerymen and reserves in the rear areas, causing over 1,600 casualties. German staff officers, impressed with the results, talked of creating "special gas batteries" controlled by special gas staffs. In the interest of flexibility, however, the high command decided that all artillery units should fire gas shells. By the war's end, gas shells comprised 50 percent of a German artillery battery's basic load.[9]

The British and French also developed gas shells with unique color codes. The French Army used these shells almost as extensively as the Germans and fired the first phosgene-filled artillery shells on 22 February 1916 at Verdun. The French also experimented with an extremely small bursting charge in order to increase the gas payload. This French innovation allowed a stable, dense cloud to form. Although the French increased the chemical payload, they erred by adding comparatively harmless *funigenes* (smoke producers), such as stannic chloride, thus reducing the toxic capacity of their phosgene shells by 30 to 40 percent.[10]

The French committed another technical error in the gas war. The hydrocyanic acid (hydrogen cyanide) used in their Vincennite shell (named for the production location) was too volatile and filled only half of the shell's capacity. Unless an extremely high concentration could be built up, there were no harmful effects. All the belligerents considered the Vincennite fill practically worthless. The French, for some reason, refused to accept this conclusion and manufactured over four million shells that, when fired, caused relatively few casualties.[11]

The British faced a constant artillery shell production shortage and supplemented their use of gas cylinders with the 4-inch Stokes mortar, introduced in July, 1916, at the Battle of the Somme. The weapon, designed specifically to fire gas and thermite shells, had a payload three times as large (six to nine pounds) as could be fired from the standard 3-inch mortar.

British artillery firing and receiving gas shells, ca 1916

A range of only 800 to 1,000 meters meant that effective delivery required emplacement in the front-line trenches. Members of the Special Brigade also experimented with a homemade contraption similar to a trench mortar.

Early in 1917 Capt. William H. Livens, a British officer, developed a device made from ordinary steel containers. This makeshift mortar fired oil drums packed with oil-soaked cotton waste. Captain Livens also began to experiment with firing large gas-filled shells from his homemade trench mortar. This resulted in a new delivery system known as the Livens projector. In its final form the projector consisted of a drawn steel cylinder eight inches in diameter, one and one-fourth inch thick, that came in two sizes—two feet nine inches or four feet long. Rounded at one end, the cylinders had a base plate that looked like a Mexican sombrero. The projectors were buried in a trench cut at a forty-five degree angle for maximum range. Originally buried to the muzzle, this depth was later found to be unnecessary, and the projectors were thereafter emplaced only deep enough to steady them for firing. The shells used with the projectors carried a payload of thirty to forty pounds of chemical agent and had a range, depending on the length of the barrel, of either 1,200 or 1,900 meters. The British first used this delivery system for what they called "gas shoots" at Arras on 4 April 1917. The Germans reported that the density of the gas delivered by this method equaled that of a gas cloud. Captured German documents claimed that the Livens projector was a deadly weapon because it not only developed a dense concentration of gas similiar to the one created

A 4-inch Stokes mortar used by British and American gas troops.

by cylinders, but like artillery, its impact came as a surprise. During the war the British fired over 300 gas projector "shoots." On 31 March 1918 the largest of these operations took place at Lens, with the firing of 3,728 of the devices.[12]

Increased casualties resulting from British gas projector attacks prompted the Germans to develop a similar weapon. Time constraints and the lack of industrial capacity for increased steel production forced them to retool their obsolete 18-cm heavy mortars. These tubes could fire a projectile containing three to four gallons of a chemical agent. In December, 1917, the Germans launched their first projector attack on the Western Front. In August, 1918, they introduced a rifled projector, 16-cm in diameter, that increased the range of the device to 3,500 meters. The shells contained thirteen pounds of chemical agent and five and one-half pounds of pumice. The pumice kept the chemical agent from being flung into the air upon explosion. It also made the agent, usually phosgene, more persistent. In one instance, the gas reportedly lingered for one and one-half hours. Yet, impressive as were these results, the Germans, despite their efforts, continued to lag behind the British in the tactical use of this delivery system.[13]

Initially, the tactical employment of chemical weapons varied to some degree between the Allies and the Central Powers; however, these variations became less noticeable during the latter stages of the war. By November, 1918, the protagonists were using similiar delivery systems and chemical agents.

Livens projector emplacement, 1918, used by British, French, and Americans.

From 1915 to 1918 the Germans held the initiative in most areas of gas warfare. They did this through the introduction of new agents that allowed them to direct more systematic thought to the question of how the employment of gas might alter a tactical situation. They were, for example, the first to use gas as an adjunct to maneuver in support of an infantry attack. The Allies struggled to keep up with such offensive doctrine, but they had to contend first with the development of effective defensive measures to counter German initiatives. Only after developing counter-measures could the Allies then plan their use of a new chemical agent or a new delivery system. This lag was evident in the case of the two most effective agents used in World War I, phosgene and mustard gas. The Germans introduced phosgene six months before the Allies were able to employ it and mustard a year ahead of their foe. The Allies had to adopt immediate defensive measures, such as effective mask filters and protective suits, before they could turn to the development of tactical doctrine. "As far as the tactical employment of gas was concerned," wrote Lt. Col. Pascal Lucas, a French officer, "it took us a long time to realize that the neutralization of personnel [by gas] could supplement the always incomplete destruction of defensive organizations" by high explosives.[14]

British gas doctrine, when circumstances did permit its development, was driven in part by a shortage of artillery shells that prohibited the British Army from mounting an artillery gas attack until the summer of 1916. In the meantime, the British, as noted, convinced themselves that chemicals released from cylinders or projectors could most effectively be used to obtain the highest possible concentration of an agent in a specific area. The consequences of this doctrine were twofold: it prevented the British from employing gas to support mobile or open warfare, and it limited the use of chemical agents primarily to the more restricted roles of attrition and harassment.

In the case of harassment, the British High Command, relying on intelligence reports, would indicate for one reason or another what German units it wished the Special Brigade to weaken or demoralize. German divisions recently transferred from the Eastern Front were prime targets because of their ignorance of defensive measures for gas warfare. The British sought out units that they expected to be transferred to the main battle fronts, i.e., Somme or Ypres, and tried to weaken them physically and psychologically before they deployed. On at least one occasion, a gas operation was postponed to await the arrival of a particular division. Once a German unit became a target for a gas attack, the Special Brigade made a point of following that unit around the front. The 1st Bavarian Regiment, for instance, was gassed fifteen times; the 1st Guards Regiment twelve times in six months; the 10th Bavarian Regiment ten times in five months, and the 9th Bavarian Regiment fourteen times from 28 June 1916 to 1 August 1917. The effects could be devastating to the morale of the gassed units and those units around them. A captured German diary recorded, "We have again had many casualties through gas poisoning. I can't think of anything worse; wherever one goes, one must take one's gas mask with one, and it will soon be more necessary than a rifle. Things are dreadful here."[15]

The British ultimately developed tactical doctrine for the use of gas shells. This doctrine set three methods for inflicting enemy gas casualties. The first and most favored method was by a surprise gas attack, in which British gunners attempted to establish the greatest concentration of gas in a target area by firing a "lavish expenditure of ammunition" at an extremely rapid rate. After one or two minutes of shelling, enemy soldiers who had not put on protective masks would be incapacitated by the dense gas; the remainder would be masked, rendering further bombardment uneconomical and unnecessary. The second method for using gas shells tried to exhaust the enemy by desultory fire over a period of many hours. In most instances, the British believed this attrition method not worth the effort, because few casualties were produced. The third method was an attempt to penetrate the enemy's gas masks with new agents such as chloropicrin, which when fired in a high concentration in a specific area, seeped into the masks and created intolerable eye irritation, coughing, vomiting, and inflammation of the respiratory tract. Enemy soldiers forced to remove their fouled masks were then subjected to a shelling with lethal phosgene.[16]

The Germans attempted to make the enemy trenches no less dreadful than their own. Having the technological advantage that gave them the ability to introduce new gases before the Allies, the Germans devoted much thought to the tactical employment of chemical weapons, and in this respect, they reached a high degree of sophistication. After abandoning cloud attacks, the Germans increased their use of gas shells. They discovered on the Eastern Front that tear gas was extremely effective in neutralizing Russian artillery. Even a few rounds would incapacitate a gun crew or, having forced it to mask, prevent it from delivering accurate fire. On the Western Front in 1916, the Germans fired some 2,000 tear gas shells at an extensive French trench system near Verdun. This massive surprise bombardment resulted in the capture of 2,400 Frenchmen who, after being temporarily blinded by the tear gas, were surrounded by German troops wearing goggles, but no masks.[17]

The Germans introduced other agents to the battlefield for specific tactical purposes. In May, 1916, they fired their Green Cross shell filled with diphosgene, a lung irritant. Later, as an indication of the increased sophistication of gas shells, they subdivided the Green Cross shell fill, first by a mix of 75 percent phosgene and 25 percent diphosgene, which was labled Green Cross 1. Then, in July, 1917, four different percentages of phosgene, diphosgene, and diphenylchlorosine called Green Cross 2, A, B, and C, respectively, were introduced. These were followed shortly by Blue Cross and Yellow Cross shells. The former shell was filled with an arsenic compound of finely separated dust. In field trials, this agent proved extremely effective in the penetration of all mask filters in existence. The need to encase the compound in a glass-lined shell, however, reduced its effectiveness, as the heat of the explosion failed to cause vaporization, and the force of the explosion caused only mechanical pulverization. The recipients, the French and British, considered Blue Cross a "failure and not worth the effort." The introduction of Yellow Cross (mustard gas), however, again gave the Germans the initiative in chemical warfare, which they held to the end of the war. By increasing the explosive charge in the shell, the Germans further extended the area contaminated by this blister producing agent. This shell was marked by a double (Lorraine) cross.[18]

The Germans found gas persisted even longer when an agent and a small amount of high explosives were placed in one shell. The effect of the high explosive, when used in the proper amount, was to spread the agent over a wider area and keep it airborne longer. With this knowledge, the Germans changed their gas doctrine from attacking a particular target to gassing large areas for extended periods of time. German staff officers began to plan operations that called for "gas barriers" and "gas pockets."

German tactical doctrine for the use of artillery gas shells offered a variety of possibilities. For the offense, it called for surprise and the concentration of as much gas as possible through the sudden and rapid placement of shells on a target area. "Cloud concentration" tactics imitated surprise tactics, but with an increase in the number of shells and an expansion of the size of a target area. Another offensive tactic was the use of gas shells that contained a high explosive charge and shrapnel. These shells, used exclusively by the Germans, had an effect "so devastating that the efficacy of a high explosive shrapnel[-gas] shell bombardment was always increased."* Once introduced, the Germans always added a percentage of these shells to any high explosive or shrapnel bombardment. The high explosive-gas shell was used extensively in German rolling barrages to support advancing infantry during the spring offenses of 1918. These shells were also used to neutralize known enemy artillery batteries and machine gun nests, thus allowing German infantry to bypass Allied strong points.[19]

The key figure in the expansion of German gas shell tactical doctrine was Lt. Col. Georg Bruchmüller, known as *"Durchbruck"* (Breakthrough) and considered an artillery genius because of his success on the battlefield. While on the Eastern Front, Bruchmüller, a great believer in the efficiency of gas shells, developed a highly sophisticated system of gas artillery fire. His tactical ideas were incorporated in the December, 1917, edition of the German manual for employment of gas shells.[20] Bruchmüller's system created "Gas Squares," which were areas known to hold enemy batteries or concentrations of enemy troops. These locations would be saturated by surprise gas shell fire, and the lethal concentration would be renewed by subsequent periodic fire. Bruchmüller's artillery tactics achieved surprise through a predicted-fire method that eliminated the usual ranging of the target by one gun of a battery. Bruchmüller formulated advanced firing

---

*Infantry troops seeking shelter from the high explosive bombardment were often forced into locations such as shell holes, where the gas settled. Furthermore, the concussion often stripped a mask off a soldier's face, exposing him to gas poisoning. More important, this tactic made Allied soldiers mask everytime they were subjected to artillery fire.

British soldiers blinded by mustard gas at an advance aid station near Béthune during the German Lys spring offensives, 9—29 April 1918.

data and tables based on meteorological variables such as wind, air temperature, and barometric pressure.[21]

When Blue Cross and Yellow Cross shells became available, Bruchmüller devised *Buntkreuz* (colored cross) tactics. One of the most successful uses of this new doctrine came on the Eastern Front, in the German crossing of the Dvina River before Riga (Map 3). On 1 September 1917 a two-hour preliminary bombardment of the Russian batteries created "varicolored zones,"* as combinations of Blue Cross and Green Cross were used both during bombardment and then during three hours of firing for effect. For the preliminary gas fire, each German battery had a set of firing sequences every twelve minutes to counter Russian batteries, which first maintained a desultory fire and then fell silent. According to German estimates, more than 116,400 gas shells were fired, which caused at least a thousand Russian casualties, mainly because of the ineffectual respirators issued to Russian troops. The figure might have been higher had not the Russians fled. German infantry reached the opposite bank to find that the Russian artillery crews had abandoned their guns in "great haste, resembling flight." The Russian infantry, which lacked effective personal protection against chemical agents, had followed suit.[22]

*Zones containing either Blue, Green, or Yellow Cross gas shells or combinations of all three.

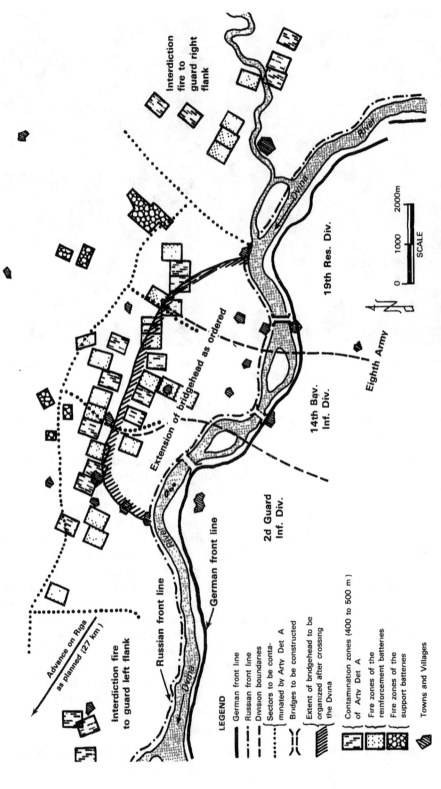

Map 3. Varicolored zones of German gas fired in support of a crossing of the Dvina River before Riga, Eastern Front, 1 September 1917.

Persistent agent fire was used tactically by the Germans on both the offense and the defense. Surprise, though desirable, was not necessary for persistent agents. Yellow Cross allowed an area to be "cleared of, or rendered inaccessible to," the enemy. Fire continued for several hours, and the contamination could be renewed each day thereafter, if so desired. The areas gassed were called "Yellow Zones of Defense." In April, 1918, the Germans shelled the city of Armentières with mustard gas (Map 4). The bombardment was so heavy that witnesses claimed liquid mustard gas ran in the streets. Naturally, the British evacuated the locale; the contamination, however, prevented the Germans from entering the city for two weeks. In the spring offensives of 1918 (Map 5), the Germans created mustard gas zones to protect the flanks of advancing infantry, to neutralize enemy strong points, to deny the enemy key terrain, to block supply routes, and to render enemy artillery batteries ineffective. "Even in open warfare," a German officer wrote, "the troops soon were asking for gas supporting fire."[23]

Mustard gas caused considerable consternation among the Allies. "We were outdistanced . . . ," a French officer noted, "the German lead on us in this respect . . . was a source of real inquietude," for the units that were exposed suffered considerably and the struggle against Yperite "seemed most deceptive of solution." The Allies eventually responded in kind, but not until June, 1918, a full year after the Germans introduced the ultimate agent of World War I, did the French use Yperite, and it took the British until 26

Various types of gas masks used in World War I.

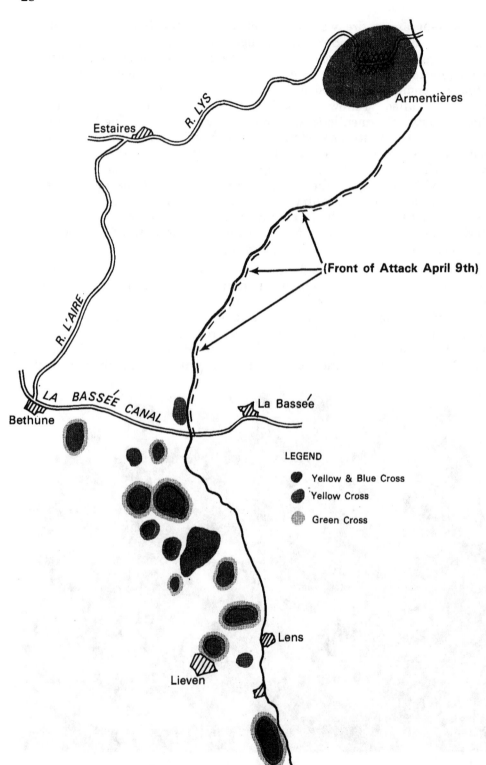

(Front of Attack April 9th)

LEGEND

⬤ Yellow & Blue Cross

⬤ Yellow Cross

⬤ Green Cross

Estaires

R. LYS

Armentières

R. L'AIRE

LA BASSÉE CANAL

Bethune

La Bassée

Lens

Lieven

Map 4.   German gas shell bombardment of Armentières on 9 April 1918.

September 1918 to retaliate with mustard. So desperate were the French to obtain the agent that British officers reported teams of French soldiers draining unexploded German Yellow Cross shells in order to reuse the gas.[24]

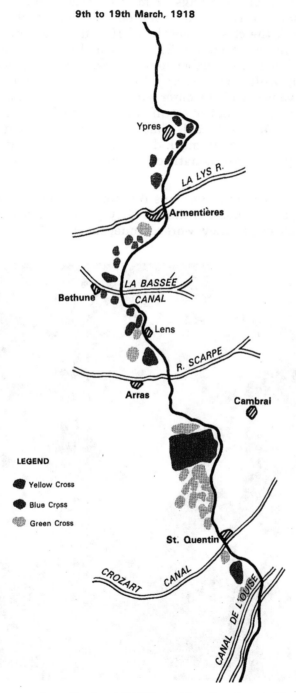

Map 5. The German spring offensives of 1918 were heavily supported by a variety of gases.

Personal protection was always a problem, one neither side ever really solved in World War I. The German High Command, prior to the first attack at Ypres, made no effort to develop an efficient gas mask. Attacking German soldiers had small protective bags of mull or hemp that were soaked in a sodium bicarbonate (baking soda) solution and then tied over the mouth and nose. Not until the closing months of 1915 did the German army begin to issue a self-contained respirator. The mask had a treated leather facepiece (because of the shortage of rubber, only officer facepieces were constructed of this material, which was more efficient than leather and easier to maintain) and eyepieces of an outer glass lens and a celluloid inner lens. The first German mask had a significant drawback: the filter had to be screwed on to the facepiece each time the mask was used, which meant that more time was required to mask during a gas attack. Later, this problem was remedied by a single construction model with a replaceable filter element.[25]

The French, British, and Russians did not coordinate their research and development of gas defenses. Although they passed information and some equipment to each other, they worked independently for the most part on

German artillerymen wearing the single-piece gas mask, early 1917.

British machine gun crew with PH-Helmets (note exhaust valve) firing during a German gas attack, Oise Sector, Marne, France, 1916.

their own protective masks.* In England, shortly after the first gas attack in April, 1915, housewives were asked by the high command to produce what became popularly known as the Black Veil Respirator—black veiling held a pad of cotton waste soaked in a chemical solution over the nose and mouth. These makeshift masks reached the British trenches in early May. When, in the latter part of 1915, the Germans began to use tear gas, the British countered with a flour sack type mask made of flannel, called the "Hypo" or "H-Helmet" after the chemical in which it was soaked, calcium hypochlorite. This mask offered protection to the eyes as well as to the respiratory system. One British officer described it as "a smoke helmet, a greasy grey-felt bag with a talc window . . . certainly ineffective against gas." This H-Helmet contained two celluloid eyepieces, but no apparatus to expel the carbon dioxide that built up in the mask.[26]

In the fall of 1915 British intelligence learned of Germany's intention to use a new gas, phosgene, a delayed-action choking agent. The Russians had also learned that the Germans intended to employ phosgene and advised the British that a solution of phenate-hexamine was effective in blocking the agent. As a result, the British soaked their H-Helmet in the Russian solution and added an outlet valve to reduce the carbon dioxide buildup inside the mask. The British Army called the new device the "PH-Helmet." The troops called it a "goggle-eyed booger with a tit."[27]

---

*This "go-it-alone" attitude, created perhaps by national pride, prevailed for most of the war in many areas besides chemical warfare. In fact, it was not until the German spring 1918 offensives that a Supreme Command came into existence to direct and coordinate the operations of the Allied armies.

French soldiers with M-2 masks advance through a gas cloud.

Although the PH-Helmet successfully blocked phosgene, it had serious drawbacks: it was hot, stuffy, and emitted an unpleasant odor; it also offered little protection against dense concentrations of lachrymatory agents. To counteract both phosgene and the lachrymating agents, the British in early 1916 took an entirely different approach to protective masks by developing a two-piece device called the "Large Box" or "Tar Box Respirator." A canister worn on the back contained neutralizing chemicals and attached by a rubber hose to a facepiece covering the chin, mouth, and nose. The wearer endured an uncomfortable noseclip and a mouthpiece similar to an athlete's rubber tooth protector. Goggles protected the eyes. The advantage of the mask rested in the use of a large filter. However, this also caused difficulties because the canister was too large and clumsy to be carried for extended distances over prolonged periods. This kind of mask reached its final stage of development with the introduction of the "Small Box Respirator" (SBR), which employed a smaller filter worn on the chest and a single construction facepiece. The details of the SBR became very familiar to men of the American Expeditionary Forces.[28]

The French wrote a different chapter to the development of the gas mask. After using the same primitive masks as the British, they set out to develop a mask that was both effective and comfortable to wear—two criteria that were, and still are, essential for the successful design of protective devices. The first significant French protective device, the M-2 mask, was similar in design to the British H-Helmet, except it did not cover the entire head, but took the form of a "snout" similar to a feedbag for a horse. Its filtration ability was limited, so French doctrine called for troops to be rotated after several hours of exposure to any gas.[29] In 1917 the French introduced the ARS (*Appareil Respiratoire Spécial*) mask. In appearance it resembled German protective equipment. The rubber facepiece had a waxed or oiled linen lining. Inhaled air passed in front of the eyepieces to prevent clouding. A canister attached to the facepiece could not be removed.

In September, 1917, these French masks were followed by another, the *Tissot*, which became one of the most effective masks of the war. As one postwar American observer noted, "the French deserve great credit" for the introduction of this defensive piece of equipment. In design, the *Tissot* was similar to the British Small Box Respirator except that the former's filter canister was carried on the soldier's back, not chest. This meant that infantrymen could carry only the *Tissot* and no other equipment. It covered the entire face, but without the uncomfortable nose clip and mouthpiece. The design allowed air to enter the mouth across the eyepieces, thus removing the normal phenomenon of condensation. The circulation of fresh air also diluted any lachrymatory gases that might enter the mask. Finally, the entire facepiece was of thin rubber. The French thought the filter location, the same as for the Large Tar Box Respirator, clumsy and difficult to adjust and, therefore, judged it unsuitable for infantry. Troops, such as artillery gun crews and stretcher bearers, who were not loaded with personal equipment and who had to continue to fight or function during a gas attack, did receive the mask. These soldiers found, in addition to comfort, that one could breathe easier and that the filtration system was superior to the ARS and M-2 mask.[30]

Unlike the British and French, the Russians devoted few resources to the development of chemical protective equipment. Consequently, they suffered the greatest number of chemically inflicted casualties in World War I. On 2 May 1915, not quite a month after the second Battle of Ypres during which French Colonial and Territorial troops collapsed under the first German gas attack, the Russians were subjected to a similar experience. German pioneer troops directed by Fritz Haber released 263 tons of chlorine gas from 12,000 cylinders against Russian troops at Bolimov. The first cylinder attack on the Eastern Front killed 6,000 Russian soldiers. Two more gas cloud attacks were made on the same position, and upward of 25,000 Russian casualties resulted. According to German sources, in June, 1915, at Bzura, two Russian regiments, the 55th and 56th Siberian, suffered approximately 9,000 gas casualties, or about 90 percent of their total strength. On 7 September 1916 a German cloud attack killed 600 Russian officers and men. The following month Transbaikal Cossacks suffered 4,000 casualties. A gas attack in 1917 cost the Russians 12 officers, 1,089 men killed, and 53 officers, 7,738 men incapacitated. Despite these casualties, the Tzarist Army developed only one mask in addition to the basic chemical-soaked gauze respirator. The fabric facepiece of this mask covered the head and attached directly to a canister containing a charcoal filter. It looked similar to the bill on a duck. Although the mask had no noseclip or mouthpiece, soldiers still found it extremely uncomfortable because the weight of the filter placed a great strain on the muscles of the neck. To make matters worse, the filter of this mask was of questionable effectiveness. By 1917 different types of British and French masks were being sent to Russia and used, to some limited extent, by Russian troops.[31]

By the summer of 1917, when U. S. troops began to arrive at French ports, chemical warfare had become commonplace and, in practice, had reached a high degree of sophistication compared to the first significant gas attack at Ypres a little over two years earlier. By July the most effective chemical agent of the war, mustard or Yellow Cross, had made its appearance. Gas shells now might contain two or even three different agents. All of the delivery systems for chemical war were in operation and efforts were being made by the combatants to improve on these weapons. The British had, for example, devised electronically detonated cylinders on tram cars for beam attacks. Also, the British had finally begun to overcome their shell production problems and had used gas shells in large quantities at the Battle of Arras in April, 1917.

Tactical doctrine for chemical warfare had reached a high level of sophistication, especially in artillery employment. In this area, the Germans, thanks to Lt. Col. Georg Bruchmüller, led the way. German artillery firing instructions became increasingly complex in regard to the selection of the gas or combination of gases to be used in a variety of tactical situations.

Given the advantage of viewing the development of chemical warfare from afar, the United States Army, upon entering the war, should have been in a position to operate in a chemical environment without repeating the costly experiences of the French, British, and Germans. Unfortunately, this was not to be the case.

The U.S. Army's Response to Chemical Warfare, 1915-1917

3

Most of the information Americans received concerning the war and chemical warfare in Europe came from the news media. Because the Royal Navy had cut the German trans-Atlantic cable early in the war, almost all news from the Continent flowed through British and French censors.

According to one author of a study on chemical warfare, Frederick Brown, Allied control of chemical warfare information to the United States can be divided into four distinct phases. During the first phase the Germans were portrayed as violators of the Hague Convention. Reports indicated that the German Army had introduced a barbaric and inhumane weapon. This line, of course, was geared to gaining support and perhaps intervention by the United States on the side of the Allies in the European war. When the French and British decided to retaliate with gas, the message changed, with Allied releases indicating that the German's first use of gas justified retaliation and the reluctant employment of similiar weapons by the Allies. A note of righteous indignation pervaded these reports, although the reports were toned down considerably when discussing the effects of gas. In the third stage, which occurred during the spring and summer of 1917, there was a total news blackout on information concerning the gas war. Assistant Secretary of War Benedict Crowell speculated on the cause. He acknowledged an increased use of chemical agents on both sides and believed the Allies "feared and perhaps with reason" that a picture of gas warfare, if presented to the Americans, would result in a "unreasonable dread of gases on the part of the American nation and its soldiers." The fourth and final phase, which came after U.S. entry into the war, was ushered in with a burst of information with virtually no censorship. The use of chemicals in this phase was depicted as a triumph of Allied technology, an example of good overcoming evil.[1]

Restricted Allied propaganda during the first three phases mentioned above impeded U.S. preparedness in chemical warfare in two ways. First, it gave U.S. officers the impression that the belligerents were making minimal use of gas and that chemical weapons, when employed, had little or no impact on the battlefield. Second, it created the perception among Army officers that chemical warfare, introduced by the barbaric Hun, was inhuman and somehow sullied the honor of the professional soldier.[2]

35

There were other reasons for the military's lack of appreciation of this new weapon. President Wilson's efforts to maintain strict neutrality during the first two years of the war hampered the Army's planning for defense. When, at one point, Wilson discovered that the General Staff's War College Division had prepared contingency plans for a war with Germany, he reprimanded Secretary of War Lindley Garrison. When the Army did tackle the problem of preparedness, chemical warfare, because it was an unfamiliar subject to most planners, received little attention. Other matters seemed more pressing. There were, for example, significant shortages of all kinds of war materiel. In 1915, the U.S. Army had only twenty-one aircraft, as compared to Britain's 250 and France's 500. The United States had fewer than 700 3-inch guns, while the French alone had 4,800 of a similar caliber prior to the outbreak of war. Based on Western Front usage, the U.S. Army had only a two-day supply of artillery shells. Similarly, four days of trench warfare would exhaust the U.S. inventory of small arms ammunition. In the assignment of priorities to overcome these and other deficiencies, chemical warfare came nowhere near the top of the list.[3]

During the summer of 1915, the U.S. Army War College published studies on the impact of the war on each belligerent's industrial base. In this report, the implications of chemical weapons and gas warfare received no notice. In November, 1915, two months after the British retaliated with gas at the Battle of Loos, the War College published a supplement to the earlier studies. This report included a survey of developments in weapons, equipment, and force structuring, but interestingly, still did not mention gas warfare.

Even the preparedness movement and the passage of the 1916 National Defense Act did nothing to spur an American assessment of the chemical war being waged in Europe. In fact, during Congressional hearings over preparedness for national defense, poison gas was mentioned only once when Col. Charles G. Treat of the U.S. Army's General Staff testified on the subject of changing artillery doctrine in Europe. Following a discussion of shrapnel shells, one Senator asked Treat, "Are they still using the poisonous gas over there, Colonel?" Treat replied, "The papers say so, but we have not had any actual reports from our observers that they are using them." In November, 1916, the same month that Treat testified, the War Department's Board of Ordnance and Fortifications noted that "certain practices" with poison gas in the European war made necessary the procurement of appropriate defensive equipment, such as gas masks for the Army. The board observed that no branch of the U.S. Army then handled anything remotely connected with chemical warfare.[4]

The board, in its final report, recommended that responsibility for the design, but not the supply, of gas masks be given to the Army's Medical Department. In reviewing the records of the board, the Adjutant General sent extracts of the comments that pertained to gas defense equipment to the Surgeon General, who concurred with the board's findings. The Chief of Staff also concurred, after which the Secretary of War gave the Surgeon General responsibility for the development and design of gas masks. No decision was made as to which branch of the Army would supply troops with protective gas equipment.[5]

The Surgeon General had detailed a number of medical officers to serve as observers with the French and British armies. Reports on the medical aspects of the European conflict, including the diagnosis and treatment of gas victims, were received by the Surgeon General from 1916 on. Unfortunately, for unexplained reasons, the Surgeon General took no action to initiate the development of protective gas devices. The Adjutant General, for his part, shelved the entire matter. Thus, on the eve of American intervention, the Army acted as if it had barely heard of chemical warfare.[6]

The Secretary of War's *Annual Report* for 1917 reflected this neglect. The report pompously declared that the "councils of prudence and forethought" should prepare the Army to surprise the enemy rather than lag "defensively behind the surprises which he prepares for us." The Secretary went on to acknowledge the tremendous impact of science on the war in Europe and referred specifically to the introduction of the airplane and the submarine. As for chemicals, he merely noted that there were other "scientific novelties" that had surfaced in the European conflict.[7]

In February, 1917, the question of the "scientific novelty" called poison gas was finally raised by an anxious Quartermaster General who pointedly asked the Adjutant General exactly which bureau of the War Department would furnish the Army with gas masks if the need arose. The question prompted the Adjutant General to initiate correspondence with the Chief of Ordnance, the Quartermaster General, and the Surgeon General to decide on the responsibility for gas mask production. At the time of the correspondence, the Surgeon General had yet to begin a program of gas mask development.[8]

That same month the Department of Interior's Bureau of Mines took the first positive steps toward preparing the Army for chemical warfare. The director, Van H. Manning, displayed a great deal more vision and foresight than did his military colleagues in Washington. At a bureau meeting, Manning asked his department chiefs what they could do to be useful if the nation should become involved in the European war. Since its founding in 1908, the bureau had investigated poison gases found in mines, conducted research on breathing devices, and examined ways to treat miners who had succumbed to noxious fumes. Obviously, this work had a direct application to chemical warfare. The day following the meeting, the Secretary of the Interior authorized Manning to contact another civilian organization, the Military Committee of the National Research Council. In a letter to C. D. Walcott, the chairman of the committee, Manning pointed out that the bureau could adapt for military application a self-contained breathing apparatus then in use for mine rescues. Also, the bureau had a test chamber at the Pittsburgh, Pennsylvania, experimental station that could be used to conduct tests on military gas masks then in use by the Europeans. The bureau hoped that the information obtained from this research could be given to the Army, allowing it to adopt the best gas mask, should the need arise.[9]

Upon receipt of this letter, Walcott arranged a meeting between representatives of the General Staff's War College Division and the Bureau of Mines. The meeting proved productive: at the end of February, 1917, the War Department accepted the bureau's offer of assistance and agreed to furnish the support, exclusive of funding, necessary to move the work along. Still, no immediate action was taken by either the Army or the Bureau of Mines to begin a defensive gas equipment research program.

On 6 April 1917, when the U.S. declared war on Germany, the Army not only lacked defensive equipment for chemical warfare, but also had no concrete plans to develop or manufacture gas masks or any other defensive equipment. Even if gas masks had been available, the Army would have had no idea how to conduct defensive gas training. Moreover, no one in the nation seemed to have any practical knowledge concerning offensive chemical warfare equipment or the doctrine then used by the Allies and the Germans for its employment.

Even after the declaration of war by Congress and the decision to ship an American division overseas, preparations for chemical warfare lacked a sense of urgency. The same day war was declared, the Council of National Defense formed a Committee on Noxious Gases. The group met in Washington and immediately adjourned to study British and French gas warfare literature. At later meetings the committee established definite guidelines for Bureau of Mines research to follow in the development of masks. Only then did the chemists at the bureau's Pittsburgh experimental station begin in earnest to develop an American gas mask. The committee also recommended that gas mask production be kept separate and distinct from research.[10]

In May, 1917, the General Staff awoke to the fact that the division requested by the French and British as a token force might well be in combat in a matter of months without any defensive gas equipment. Maj. L. P. Williamson, liaison officer between the Bureau of Mines and the War Department, received a directive from the General Staff telling him to seek the bureau's assistance in the manufacture of 25,000 gas masks. George A. Burrell,* a civilian chemist in the bureau's Research Laboratory, "readily and willingly accepted" the task, but not, as he later noted, "fully appreciating all the conditions which a war mask had to encounter." Burrell should not have been so hard on himself. No one in the United States really understood or even knew much about the employment of chemical defensive equipment on the battlefield.[11]

Working day and night, employees of four different civilian companies fabricated 20,088 masks and filters, using a British Small Box Respirator (SBR) as a model. The masks were shipped overseas to be examined and tested by British experts. They were quickly rejected. The British cabled

*Burrell was made a colonel in the Corps of Engineers and later served in the Chemical Warfare Service Research Division.

back that the masks were unacceptable for combat because the mouthpiece was too large and stiff. They also found the rubberized cloth facepiece did not filter out the agent chloropicrin, which was then being used by the Germans in increasing quantities. The filter, which was worn on the chest in a container, had soda-lime granules that were too soft. With repeated jolting, the granules would clog the canister and increase resistance to breathing.

While this was going on, the acting Chief of Staff, Maj. Gen. Tasker Bliss, after a lengthy round of memoranda initiated by the Adjutant General, informed the Surgeon General on 16 May 1917 that, in addition to research and development, the Medical Department would be responsible for supplying the U.S. Army with gas masks and other defensive equipment. During the next fiscal year the Medical Department would be responsible for supplying 1,000,000 gas masks, 8,500 decontamination sprayers for use in trench warfare, and 1,000 oxygen resuscitators for the treatment of chemical casualties. Unfortunately, neither the Chief of Staff nor the Surgeon General created an office to procure the equipment. The Surgeon General did, however, assign an officer to the National Research Council's Committee on Noxious Gases.[12]

The Committee on Noxious Gases soon met with representatives from the Army and Navy and with members of a French scientific mission. After several sessions, the committee sent a memorandum to the Secretary of War on 2 July 1917, informing him that it had worked out a partial organization plan for a "gas service." Unfortunately, the use of the term "gas service" was misleading, because what the committee recommended turned out to be a cumbersome decentralized system for preparing the Army for chemical warfare. The offensive aspects of gas warfare, the committee explained, should be handled by the Ordnance Department, the defensive measures by the Medical Department. The Bureau of Mines would continue to direct research, and the Corps of Engineers would receive responsibility for handling all chemical warfare material on the battlefield. The General Staff immediately put this decentralized system into effect.[13]

On 24 July 1917 the Chief of Staff ordered the Medical Department to provide nine officers as instructors for a Gas Defense School to be organized at the Infantry School of Musketry, Fort Sill, Oklahoma. As a result of this order, the Medical Department received the additional responsibility for the conduct of defensive gas training. Medical officers with absolutely no experience in gas warfare were now expected to train other medical officers for duty as instructors for an Army that would eventually be expanded to over three million men.[14]

After an interminable delay, the Surgeon General on 31 August 1917 finally created a Gas Defense Service composed of three sections: Field Supply, Overseas Repair, and Training. He placed a Medical Corps officer in command and filled his staff with members of the Medical Department's Sanitary Corps.* The officers had no chemical warfare doctrine to guide

*The Sanitary Corps is equivalent to today's Medical Service Corps.

them. Only two War Department publications existed in the United States to assist these gas officers: a hurriedly compiled *Notes on Gas as a Weapon in Modern War* and a *Memorandum on Gas Poisoning in Warfare*. Both publications appear to have borrowed extensively from French and British gas warfare doctrine, some of it outdated.[15]

The creation of a Training Section, even with its limited expertise, came none too soon. In September, 1917, draftees, volunteers, and National Guardsmen began to arrive at the thirty-six training cantonments scattered across the country. Sanitary Corps and division medical officers, with only several thousand masks at their disposal (including the 20,088 rejected by the British), faced the overwhelming task of training hundreds of thousands of troops in gas warfare and gas defense. Shortages of equipment, manuals, and knowledge were not the only problems facing the new gas officers. Gas was such a new weapon that division commanders and their staff officers were unwilling to give up training time for chemical defense at the expense of more traditional military skills such as close order drill and marksmanship. It was a wonder that any defensive training in gas warfare took place. Many times it did not. Initially, there were at best one or two hours of gas defense lectures, sometimes accompanied by a demonstration of how to wear the gas mask.[16]

The lack of knowledge and experience with gas bred "ignorance and superstition" among recruits and veterans alike. Rumors swept through the camps that Germany had "a gas that would make [soldiers'] eyes drop out of their sockets or their fingers and toes drop off." To the unsophisticated youths who filled the training camps, "gas was mysterious enough, but add to it the word chemical, and it became hopelessly beyond . . . their conception." Gas was such an "intangible thing," a division commander noted, that a level of understanding adequate to guard against the dangers it posed was difficult to reach. Reaching such a level continued to be a hopeless task because no coherent U.S. gas warfare doctrine existed. As a consequence, a majority of World War I doughboys found themselves in a chemical combat environment with only a minimal amount of defensive gas training and with "no idea of what this training really meant."[17]

Confronted with this unfortunate situation, the War College of the General Staff examined the evolving gas defense program in the fall of 1917. Defensive training in gas warfare—regardless of how rudimentary—had to be given to men going to Europe. Ypres had proved what chemical warfare could do to unprepared soldiers. Severe casualties and battlefield defeat might well occur if immediate steps were not taken to train men in the defensive aspects of chemical warfare. As a result, the War College requested and received a British gas officer and a gas NCO for each of the thirty-six training cantonments.

In late October, 1917, the British gas experts arrived in the United States. Their activities were coordinated and directed by Maj. S. J. M. Auld, Special Brigade, Royal Engineers.* Auld quickly made his presence felt. Impressed

*The British Special Brigade of the Royal Engineers was an offensive gas unit. (See Chapter 2.)

by the British gas officer's knowledge and practical experience, the War College and the Field Training Section asked him to prepare "a working textbook on gas" in order to fill the U.S. Army's doctrinal void in chemical warfare. Working with Sanitary Corps Capt. James H. Walton, Auld wrote four pamphlets that were later combined as Adjutant General Document 705, *Gas Warfare*. They were initially published individually in the following order:

Part Three: *Methods of Training in Defensive Methods*

Part Two: *Methods of Defense Against Attack*

Part One: *German Methods of Offense*

Part Four: *The Offensive in Gas Warfare — Cloud and Projector*

Thus, British gas warfare doctrine edited by the War College Division of the General Staff became U.S. Army doctrine.[18]

Auld strongly influenced the organization of the U.S. Army for chemical warfare in one other way. When he and other British officers discovered that the General Staff had placed defensive training under the Medical Department, they were appalled. The British officers insisted that gas defense was "purely a military affair"; in their opinion, proper defensive measures were "largely a question of discipline." Based on the experience of the British Army, such procedures were so closely connected with the soldier's "fighting activities" that preparation for chemical warfare could not be carried out by a noncombat branch of the Army. The British were so emphatic that, in January, 1918, by order of the General Staff, the Field Training Section of the Sanitary Corps passed to the Corps of Engineers.[19]

Major Auld also suggested the establishment of a Central Army Gas School to train "Divisional, Brigade and Regimental Gas officers and other personnel whom it might be desirable to educate in Gas Warfare." This idea was already under consideration by the General Staff. The result was the establishment of an Army Gas School at Camp A. A. Humphreys, Virginia,* where in May, 1918, two initial courses began. The first, a four-day course for officers and noncommissioned officers, provided general information on gas warfare. The second, a twelve-day course, was for Chief Gas Officers who would be assigned to division and higher echelon staffs. Although there were similarities between the two courses, the Chief Gas Officers' instruction went into greater detail on most matters. The shortage of trained gas officers in the AEF prevented students from being held for longer periods of field training on subjects such as gas detection, construction of gas-proof dugouts, and the proper wearing of respirators.[20]

Auld assisted in training the first U.S. gas officers, forty-five first lieutenants, all chemists, who were assigned to the Field Training Section of the Sanitary Corps.**The instruction took place at the American University

*Later, in October, 1918, the Army Gas School was moved to Camp Kendrick, adjacent to Lakehurst, New Jersey, the proving ground for the new Chemical Warfare Service established on 11 May 1918.

**In January, 1918, the General Staff placed the Sanitary Corps' Field Training Section under the Corps of Engineers.

Recruits undergoing a simulated gas attack at a National Army Camp, 1918.

in Washington, DC. In January, 1918, after three months of training in gas warfare and general military subjects, thirty-three of the forty-five officers, together with their British instructors, departed for duty at division training camps. The other twelve went directly to France. Unfortunately, by January, 1918, six of the thirty U.S. divisions destined to see combat in France had either left the States or had completed training. The men in these units had received no chemical warfare training before embarking for Europe. As for the divisions that did receive some training before shipping overseas, their division gas officers were afterwards assigned to the 473d Engineer Regiment, a stateside administrative holding unit. Thus, the first trained gas officers did not deploy with the men they hau trained. Although necessary for the training of subsequent divisions, this decision had, in the words of one gas officer, a "discouraging effect upon the men and upon gas training and discipline in general" in the unit deployed overseas. The confidence of the embarking troops was hardly bolstered when the "experts" on chemical warfare stayed home.

As the war progressed, the training in the division camps improved. In January, 1918, the 29th Division's gas training at Camp McClellan consisted of a brief lecture and gas mask drill for one hour daily, five days a week, under the close supervision of British instructors. This compared favorably to the weekly one-hour "anti-gas instruction" in October, 1917. As training became more sophisticated, men underwent tests at the end of their division's training cycle. They masked and entered a chamber filled with chlorine gas. Next, they went through a chamber filled with a tear agent, where they unmasked. Although by the summer of 1918, recruits received standardized chemical warfare training, reports filed by division gas officers in Europe indicated the key to successful preparation had yet to be found. Still more training was needed, and it had to be integrated with other subjects.[21]

In the summer of 1918, with news reaching America of Germany's increased use of gas, an Army regulation was promulgated, requiring every doughboy who left the country to have a certificate indicating he had completed gas training. No other military skill required such validation. Unfortunately, the requirement was usually ignored, and most men continued to arrive in France without the benefit of adequate instruction in gas defense. Gas officers realized that sufficient time for training in the camps did not exist. To make up for the deficiency, units attempted to use the time aboard transports for defensive gas training. The 80th Division, for example, ordered that shipboard activities would include physical training, manual of arms, guard duty, and "anti-gas instruction."[22]

Although the U.S. Army's first efforts in chemical warfare were directed toward "anti-gas" or defensive measures, the development of the means to retaliate in kind soon followed. On 15 August 1917, with the approval of the General Staff in Washington, AEF General Order 108 authorized the organization of special and technical engineer troops that would be assigned to each army as a "Gas and Flame" Regiment.* The War Department ordered recruits for the newly formed 30th Engineers to report to the American University campus in Washington, DC, where they were transformed into

*"Flame" disappeared from the name and from use when GHQ, AEF, decided that the primitive flamethrowers used by the British and the French were more dangerous to the operator than to the enemy.

the 1st Gas Regiment. Unfortunately, with no one to instruct them in offensive or even defensive gas warfare, the only training the first companies of the gas regiment received in the United States involved close order drill. The unit underwent no special training in gas warfare. Beginning in December, 1917, the companies of the 1st Gas Regiment left the United States without gas masks.[23]

Recruits at Camp Kearney, California, using British Ayrton or trench fans to clear gas, 1918.

The gas mask problem continued to plague the Army as a whole. An effective American mask was eventually developed using the British Small Box Respirator as a model. However, production of American gas masks peaked just one month prior to the end of the war. Late delivery and the initial small number of masks produced were offset only by the AEF's decision to purchase several million British and French gas masks.[24]

The same unpreparedness and production lag applied to offensive chemical weapons. The Army attempted to contract out the production of war gases to a number of civilian chemical companies, but these firms objected immediately to the contracts because of the inherent dangers in the production of large quantities of war gases and because the demand for the product would not extend beyond the conflict. Besides that, the firms had already overcommitted their plants and personnel for the production of other war-related chemical products.[25]

The Army thus found itself with no alternative but to construct its own production facilities. In December, 1917, construction of plants to produce chemical agents began at Gunpowder Neck, Maryland. By the summer of 1918, the Edgewood Arsenal there had plants in operation producing phosgene, chloropicrin, mustard, chlorine, and sulfur trichloride. The arsenal also had a capability for filling artillery shells, although most of the agents produced were shipped overseas to the Allies in fifty-five gallon drums. Because of insufficient time, not one single gas shell manufactured at the arsenal ever reached an American artillery piece in France. When production of chemicals finally peaked one month prior to the Armistice, the plants had to stop production for lack of shell casings. AEF artillery units and special gas troops fired American produced war gas, but in French and British shells.[26]

As the emphasis on chemical warfare increased, there arose a need to coordinate the various agencies assigned responsibility for gas warfare. Accordingly, on 28 June 1918 President Wilson, using the authority given to him by the Overman Act,* ordered the establishment of the Chemical Warfare Service (CWS) as a separate branch of the National Army. Immediately, all activities pertaining to chemical warfare were placed under Maj. Gen. William L. Sibert, formerly Commanding General of the First Infantry Division. The creation of a branch of the Army dedicated to chemical warfare was significant because it acknowledged, albeit belatedly, the tremendous impact the new weapon was having on the AEF.[27]

The CWS, with the concurrence of the General Staff, established ten subordinate divisions:

- Administration
- Research
- Gas Defense
- Gas Offense
  (Edgewood Arsenal)
- Development

- Proving
- Medical
- Training
- Overseas
  (Gas Service, AEF)
- 1st Gas Regiment

With the exception of the Overseas Division and the 1st Gas Regiment, the division chiefs were located in Washington, DC, and the operations of their divisions were scattered throughout the United States. The Administration Division facilitated routine matters and coordinated the activities of the other CWS divisions. A Research Division, as the name implied, handled all basic research, from the discovery of new chemicals to the development of protective masks and offensive equipment. Another division, Gas Defense,

*The Overman Act of 20 May 1917 gave the president the authority to reorganize executive agencies during the war emergency.

conducted research, but primarily administered the manufacturing, testing, and inspecting of gas masks for men and animals. This division also had the responsibility for manufacturing gas-proof dugout blankets, protective suits and gloves, antigas ointment, and "gas warning" signals. The Gas Defense Division administered Edgewood Arsenal. A Development Division experimented with charcoal suitable for gas mask filters, a manufacturing process for mustard, and a means of producing casings and adapters for 75-mm shells of similar design to the French glass-lined gas projectiles. A Proving Division tested prototype gas shells before production and spot-tested shells prior to shipment overseas. The Medical Division coordinated work on the therapy, pharmacology, physiology, and pathology of war gases on the body. This division's primary emphasis was on the prevention and treatment of casualties from mustard gas.[28]

The agency that had its most direct impact on the AEF was the Chemical Warfare Service's Training Division. The division's responsibilities included the organization and training of gas troops, the training of "casual detachments for overseas duty," the maintenance of a Chemical Warfare Training Camp detachment, and the procurement and training of chemical officers for overseas duty. In recognition of the division's importance, the Assistant Director of the Chemical Warfare Service, Brig. Gen. H. C. Newcomer, assumed operational command. This was the only division, other than Administration, headed by a general officer.

The structure of the CWS in the United States was determined by the personnel and equipment requirements of the AEF. Stateside training and preparations for chemical warfare had to be curtailed in order to rush American troops to France. Initially, expertise in chemical warfare was lacking. As a consequence, combat divisions deployed without proper training, equipment, and leadership. Until late 1917, there was no chemical warfare doctrine to rely upon. Nevertheless, American troops had to fight on a chemical battlefield against an opponent highly skilled in the use of chemicals in combat. Out of necessity it fell to the Overseas Division, CWS, to bear the brunt of the responsibility for preparing American soldiers for chemical warfare.

The majority of the thirty AEF divisions to see combat in World War I entered the line during and after the five German spring offensives of 1918. These offensives saw chemical warfare at the highest level since its introduction three years before. Regardless of the emphasis eventually placed on gas warfare by GHQ, AEF, and the Army General Staff, new doctrine for gas weapons could not be fully absorbed or mastered by the inexperienced Americans. Prewar neglect of gas warfare equipment and accompanying doctrine had a significant impact on the ability of the AEF to defend against, and to successfully employ, chemical agents in World War I.

The AEF Organizes for Chemical Warfare

On 13 June 1917, while the General Staff in the United States struggled to organize, man, and equip an army, General John J. Pershing, Commander of the American Expeditionary Forces (AEF), arrived in France with a staff of fifty-three officers and 146 enlisted men. After a continuous round of official visits and ceremonies, Pershing and his staff settled into temporary headquarters in Paris. Two weeks later the first American troops arrived in France. General Order 8, published on 5 July 1917, established the organization of the AEF General Headquarters (GHQ). This order also created on paper the GHQ position of "Chief of the Gas Service," whose responsibilities included procurement of gas personnel and supplies, the "conduct of the entire Gas and Flame Service both offense and defense," the supervision of training for gas officers and troops, and experimentation with new gases, delivery systems, and protective devices.[1]

Ordering the creation of a Gas Service was a simple matter. The actual organizing of a new branch of the Army, however, would take a tremendous amount of effort and time. Time was precious. By mid-July, over 12,000 doughboys were within thirty miles of the front, all without gas masks or training in chemical warfare. Yet, because of more pressing problems,* it was not until 17 August 1917 that General Pershing sent a cable to Washington requesting the organization of a Gas Service and the authority to appoint Lt. Col. Amos A. Fries, Corps of Engineers, as its chief.

Lieutenant Colonel Fries had arrived in France three days earlier. As an engineer officer he was assigned responsibility for organizing a road network to support the AEF Services of Supply (SOS). Several days later Col. Hugh A. Drum and Col. Alvin B. Barber of the GHQ, AEF, approached Fries. As Fries recalled after the war, the staff officers asked what "I should think if my orders were changed so as to make me Chief of the newly proposed gas service." Given overnight to decide, Fries accepted. On 22 August 1917 he began to build an organization based on information Barber and Drum had compiled about the British Special Brigade and French "Z"

---

*In addition to commanding an army in a combat zone, Pershing was faced with the same problems that the General Staff in Washington had—the officering, billeting, feeding, equipping, and training of a vast army of raw recruits.

units. In addition, the staff officers gave Fries a draft of a proposed General Order 31 that would establish a Gas Service.[2]

General Order 31 assigned the Gas Service responsibility for both offensive and defensive operations, including the organization of gas personnel, gas warfare supplies, and gas warfare training in the AEF. Appended to the order was a draft chart of the Gas Service Organization. In reviewing the chart with Fries, Pershing noted that the offensive arm included Stokes mortar companies. This prompted him to ask why existing trench mortar companies could not be utilized to fire gas rounds. Barber and Drum, who were also present, explained that gas operations were too technical and dangerous for untrained personnel to conduct and, therefore, required special troops. They also told Pershing that in the British Army the Special Brigade used 4-inch Stokes mortars.[3]

Acting on Pershing's instructions, Fries, with Colonel Church and Captain Boothby of the Medical Department, visited the British Special Brigade headquarters at St.Omer. Church had served as an observer with the French Army for a year and a half and, during that time, had collected information on chemical warfare defense. Boothby did the same while observing British chemical warfare procedures and also took a course at the British defense school. At St.Omer the medical officers discussed British defensive gas doctrine, while Fries obtained information on the offensive aspects of chemical warfare. Fries elicited information on gases in use, special troops, chemical ammunition, and delivery systems. He also visited the large chemical material depot for the British Fifth Army.

After returning to AEF headquarters, the three officers reviewed both the draft General Order and the organizational chart. They modified the original proposals to provide general rather than specific guidelines, anticipating that only actual combat experience would glean the information necessary to build a truly effective organization. Fries criticized the British system that divided responsibility for offensive and defensive gas warfare. Paradoxically, the British liaison officer in the United States, Maj. S. M. J. Auld, warned the Americans against just such a practice. Thus, the AEF Gas Service made it the responsibility of all gas officers to be knowledgeable in both areas, a point driven home in subsequent general orders detailing the duties of army, corps, and division gas officers. On 3 September 1917, almost five months after the United States entered the war, the final version of General Order 31 was published (Figure 2).[4]

Not until 27 May 1918, as U.S. divisions were coming on-line in increasing numbers and experiencing heavy gas casualties, did GHQ, AEF, issue General Order 79 for the establishment of unit gas officers. Only then did Fries have the authority to appoint chief gas officers for armies and corps and gas officers and assistants for divisions. Until this time, division commanders had been appointing gas officers as they saw fit. Under the new arrangements, chief gas officers of armies and corps and division gas officers would be staff officers responsible to the commander. Parallel reporting procedures were established in order to ensure that accurate information

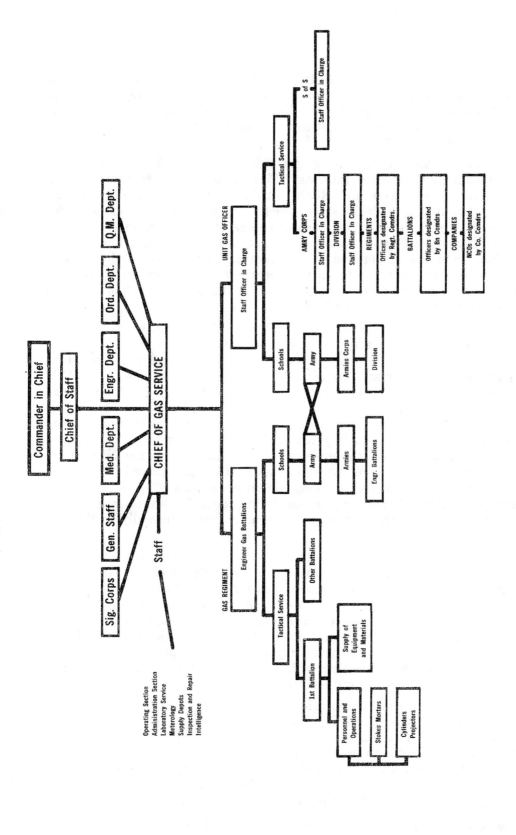

Figure 2. Organization of the Gas Service, AEF, 1917.

reached the proper authorities. In addition to reports through official channels, the order authorized these officers to send required reports directly to the Chief of the Gas Service. The Chief, with GHQ approval, could also order these unit staff officers to attend meetings necessary for the coordination of defensive gas measures.

The division and higher echelon gas officers had specific duties assigned. By direction of their commanding officers, they were to instruct and supervise the gas officers and NCOs within their command, supervise all defensive training and drill, collect enemy chemical warfare material for submission to AEF laboratories, inspect defensive measures, and advise the commander and staff regarding all aspects of chemical warfare. The division gas officer had the responsibility of reporting to the commander all gas casualties and actions taken to prevent recurrences. The division commander forwarded this report, together with a list of the actions he had taken to correct the deficiencies, to the Chief of the Gas Service.

Regimental and battalion commanders assigned duties to their gas officers. At this level, gas officer and gas NCO responsibilities were considered additional, not primary duties. A gas officer and NCO assistant were required for regiment, battalion, and separate units, and two NCOs were appointed for each company. Selected on the basis of undefined "special qualifications," the men were trained at the AEF Gas Defense School or corps gas schools. Among their duties, they supervised training in the use of gas masks, gas proof shelters, alarm systems, and related defensive measures. When the division entered combat, the gas NCOs were required to inspect all defensive equipment and antigas procedures at least twice a week. They reported weather, terrain conditions, all new enemy gas tactics and material, and any noted deficiencies. This information was reported officially to the company commander and informally to the battalion commander.

General Order 79 established an AEF Gas Defense School with a course of instruction "adequate for the training in gas defense of gas officers and noncommissioned officers." The school director received specific instructions to coordinate his activities with those of officers engaged in offensive gas instruction and with those at the AEF's new chemical experimental station at Hanlon Field near Chaumont. Instructors at the Gas Defense School kept abreast of the latest changes in gas warfare by personally reviewing files of Allied and American gas officer reports and by reading translated copies of captured German and Austrian documents.

General Order 79 dealt primarily with the Gas Corps* and the training of its officers, but it also called the attention of "all ranks" to the "increasing importance of gas warfare." Although the Gas Corps would do everything that was possible to prepare individuals and units to avoid casualties from gas, the "ultimate responsibility" for defense against gas, the order concluded, "devolves upon commanding officers" who must provide for the training of their men and the maintenance of gas discipline. In order to

*Gas Service and Gas Corps were terms used interchangeably in the AEF.

maintain gas discipline and provide adequate training, the order urged commanders to cooperate with Gas Corps officers.[5]

The extensive use of gas by the Germans in their spring 1918 offensives caused the AEF General Staff to expand the duties of gas officers. As of 2 July 1918, gas officers were to be consulted and their technical knowledge utilized in the preparation of all plans involving the extensive use of gas, whether by artillery or other means. Thus, the duties and responsibilities of gas officers grew with the increasing awareness of the impact chemical agents were having on the offensive and defensive capabilities of AEF units. Fries, however, faced a chronic problem of locating competent men to serve in a branch of service that lacked precedent and had an unknown future. This was further complicated by an Armywide shortage of personnel. The Corps of Engineers, originally the primary source of gas officers, became reluctant, as its own demand for officers grew, to have men reassigned to another branch.[6]

The AEF Gas Service had other problems with which to contend. There was, for example, a severe shortage of gas warfare supplies. The lack of protective masks for members of the AEF caused the greatest concern. On 2 August 1917, GHQ, AEF decided to utilize the British Small Box Respirator (SBR) as its primary mask and the French M-2 mask* as an "emergency" protective device.[7]

The SBR consisted of a canister-type filter of absorbent charcoal with alternating layers of oxidized soda lime granules. A flexible rubber tube connected the canister to a rubberized facepiece that was held to the face by elastic bands in order to provide an airtight fit. Inside the facepiece was a rubber nose clip. A hard rubber mouthpiece that the wearer grasped by his teeth was connected to the flexible hose attached to the filtration canister. A soldier exhaled air through a rubber flutter valve at the front of the mask. The wearer viewed the world through two lenses made of celluloid or specially prepared glass. Each soldier had a tube of "anti-dimming" or defogging paste that could be used to prevent condensation from forming on the lenses. Lacking an American mask, the AEF placed an initial order for 600,000 SBRs and 100,000 French M-2 masks. Additional orders followed, as it would take the United States a year from its entry into the war to begin providing its troops in the field with an acceptable American-made version of the SBR.[8]

The shortage of respirators notwithstanding, no individual could enter the combat zone unless equipped with a mask. Commanders and staff officers went to considerable lengths to ensure that all members of their units had respirators. In late December, 1917, the newly arrived 42nd "Rainbow" Division was moved by rail to a training site in France. On the train were masks for the unit, which the division's Chief of Staff planned to issue on its arrival. The 1st Division, however, was due to go "on the

---

*Because of its poor filtration capability and flimsy construction, the M-2 mask was later banned for use in the alert zone for everyone except men with head wounds who could not wear the SBR, men who were unconscious and could not grasp the mouthpiece, and black soldiers who could not wear the nose clips of the SBR.

line shortly" and submitted an urgent request for respirators. The Chief of the Gas Service responded by ordering the 42nd's Chief of Staff to transfer his masks to the 1st Division. To circumvent the order, the 42nd's Chief of Staff immediately stopped the train and ordered the masks issued to his men. He then reported to Fries that it was impossible to comply with the order because the masks had already been issued.[9]

Several thousand men of the 1st Division lacked masks, and its 1st Brigade was scheduled to move to the front line in January.* Fries finally obtained a "priority of shipment" and detailed several gas officers to accompany the masks from Le Havre, the major British supply base, to ensure their safe delivery to the 1st Division. Despite these precautions, one carload of 4,000 masks disappeared in transit. Fries finally had to order the 2nd Brigade of the 1st Division to turn in their SBRs. These were cleaned and reissued to the Division's 1st Brigade. This episode was not an isolated one.[10]

Gas equipment and supplies in the United States and France were initially the responsibility of the nearest related branch of the Army. The AEF Gas Service found this procedure "exceedingly embarrassing, cumbersome and inefficient." Despite initial resistance, the General Staff in Washington approved AEF requisition submitted on 10 September 1917 for 50,000 cylinders, 50,000 Livens projector shells, and a large quantity of Stokes mortars and ammunition. None of these weapons or ammunition reached the AEF in time to be used in combat. To avoid duplication of effort and to save time, Fries, in February, 1918, received permission to make direct purchases of equipment from the Allies. At that time almost all of the gas warfare material used by the AEF came from the British. Not until April, 1918, did any material manufactured in the United States begin to reach the AEF. As noted in the preceding chapter, a number of war gases were manufactured in the United States during the war, and more than 3,600 tons of these did reach the French and British.[11]

Because of a shortage of artillery pieces, artillery units of the AEF were equipped primarily with the French 75-mm light field gun, the 155-mm medium howitzer, and the 240-mm heavy howitzer, as well as with British 8-inch and 9.2-inch heavy howitzers. The U.S. Army also adopted, with minor modifications, the French gas shell. The AEF Services of Supply purchased French shells and painted them according to an American color code.**[12]

Originally, the SOS defensive gas equipment fell into Class I with clothing, leather goods, and optical instruments. In February, 1918, when the Gas Service was given authority to requisition its own supplies, all

---

*Only one-half of the 1st Division was needed to relieve a French division (French divisions were one-half the size of the comparable American unit). The balance of the 1st Division remained in training.

**They were distinguished by a gray body lettered "Special Gas." A strip colored either white or red or both circled the shell. Nonpersistent gas had only red, semipersistent gas combined red and white. The number of stripes indicated the relative persistency, the least persistent having fewer stripes.

items of gas warfare equipment were placed into a new category, Class V. In September, 1918, the Army created four subclasses within the general Class V classification. Subclass A material included offensive gas supplies, such as gas shells and grenades, that were not used by gas troops but by the combat arms. Subclass B material included those gas supplies issued exclusively to gas troops. Subclass C supplies encompassed aviation, smoke, and incendiary material. Subclass D items included all defensive gas material. The Ordnance Corps transported and issued subclasses A and C, while the Gas Service did the same for B and D items. The Gas Service distributed all "anti-gas supplies." Fries ordered a 10 percent reserve of all equipment at the division gas dumps, and each company or regiment maintained a 5 percent reserve supply. The division gas officer issued the required masks to the regimental supply officers, who distributed them to battalions. Gas officers also issued gas alarm devices, Strombo horns, Klaxon horns, and gongs directly to company commanders in each sector. Later, army and corps gas officers were given similar responsibility for the issue of gas supplies to corps artillerymen and all rear echelon troops.[13]

Another branch heavily involved in chemical warfare was the Army's Medical Department. The General Staff anticipated that medical officers would require some knowledge of the actual symptoms brought on by chemical agents and the various methods of treatment for gas poisoning. Consequently, in May, 1917, the War Department issued a "Memorandum on Gas Poisoning in Warfare with Notes on Its Pathology and Treatment," based on British sources. Still, despite this assistance from Washington, most of the planning and organization for the treatment of gas casualties was done by the AEF in France.[14]

Maj. J. R. Church, Medical Department, was the first Medical Director of the Gas Service in France. While on the General Staff, he had assisted in the initial planning for an AEF Gas Service. As Medical Director he devoted most of his time to organizational matters. The increase in gas casualties, however, resulted in a personnel change in the position, with Lt. Col. Harry L. Gilchrist, M.D., the former commander of Number 9, General Hospital, replacing Church. Gilchrist prepared for his new assignment by attending the British Gas School at Rouen, France.[15]

When Gilchrist reported for duty as Medical Director, he found no records or guidelines detailing the responsibilities of his position. His first priority, and one agreed to by Fries, was to launch a gas instruction campaign directed specifically at AEF medical officers. On 9 February 1918, Gilchrist published a pamphlet, "Symptomology, Pathology and General Treatment of Gas Cases," which provided medical officers basic information on the treatment of chemical casualties. Following this publication, the Medical Director's office issued a constant stream of bulletins aimed at keeping AEF medical officers up-to-date on the latest medical developments in gas warfare. Gilchrist visited most AEF divisions and hospitals, where he lectured to officers and men on chemical warfare from a medical point of view, emphasizing prevention and treatment of gas casualties.[16]

As the chemical war escalated with the introduction of mustard gas, the Medical Director's responsibilities and, indeed, his department's tasks became increasingly crucial to the AEF. Gilchrist inspected troops at the front and visited medical personnel in hospitals, hospital trains, and other locations. He also served as the liaison officer between the Gas Service and the Medical Department, advising both the AEF's Chief of the Gas Service and the Chief Surgeon on gas-related medical matters. In addition to these general duties, he collected all medical information relating to gas warfare and relayed it to the AEF's Chief Surgeon. Gilchrist focused his attention on such matters as new treatment for gas casualties and "combating the effects of the enemy gases not only from a therapeutic, but also from a prophylactic point of view." To obtain information, he visited the sites of battles where large numbers of gas casualties had occurred.[17]

Because armies and corps of the AEF were formed after the arrival of a number of divisions, the medical structure to treat gas casualties evolved first within the division. On 1 March 1918, the 42nd Division became the second American division to occupy a sector on the Western Front. Although initially the division had few gas casualties, the medical officers prepared for a large influx of gas victims. All four of the division's field hospitals were set up to accept gas victims, and orders were given that a total of 500 beds be put aside for such cases. On 20 March the Germans launched an artillery bombardment of mustard and high explosive shells that hit the 42nd Division's 165th Infantry at 1730 hours. In the space of a few minutes, the mustard caused 270 casualties, including one death. The first-aid station through which the casualties passed also received a drenching with gas, so medical personnel wore masks as they treated the patients.[18]

As a result of this attack and others that followed, the 42nd Division took several steps to improve the treatment of gas casualties. These later became standard for AEF divisions in the line. The first measure was to dedicate one of the four division field hospitals to gas cases. The position of division Gas Medical Officer was also created. Memorandum 148, HQ, 42nd Division, published on 23 April 1918, listed the duties of this officer as the instruction of medical personnel in gas defense; the supervision of gas protection of medical dugouts, aid stations, and field hospitals; the early diagnosis of symptoms; and the treatment of all types of gas casualties.[19]

The AEF adopted the 42nd Division's practices when it instituted the position of division Gas Medical Officer in AEF General Order 144, dated 29 August 1918. GHQ took this measure in the face of mounting gas casualties and a high incident of gas malingering. As a consequence, in addition to the duties indicated in the 42nd Division's memorandum, the AEF order added duties such as the instruction of all division personnel on the early symptoms and treatments of gas poisoning and the instruction of line officers in practical medical matters connected with gas warfare. The orders stated that any officers selected must be "live, wide-awake, energetic men, and must show a keen appreciation of the work." By the first week in October, 1918, each AEF division had a Gas Medical Officer. These men were sent to the School of Pharmacy's School of Gas (*Ecole de Gaz*) at the University of Paris for a four-day course to prepare them for their division duties.[20]

Beyond the division field hospitals, each army established its own gas hospitals.* The first such installation began operation on 29 August 1918. Army-level hospital personnel were casuals, or officers and men loaned from base or evacuation hospitals or anywhere else medical personnel could be found. To meet the demands of the Meuse-Argonne offensive, the Chief Surgeon, AEF, in September, 1918, established five gas hospitals with a total of 1,650 beds. Colonel Gilchrist suggested three mobile 1,500-bed gas hospitals be established, one for each U.S. corps. This plan, however, was never implemented because of insufficient personnel. Another plan called for the creation of two "emergency gas teams" to be assigned to each base hospital. Their mission was to "relieve the strain" that sudden gas attacks put on division field hospitals. The GHQ, AEF, organized several "emergency gas teams," each consisting of a medical officer, two nurses, and two orderlies. The Chief Surgeon of the 1st U.S. Army, Col. A. N. Stark, however, objected to these teams on the grounds that base hospitals were too far removed from the fighting. He also believed that the division field hospitals set aside for gassed soldiers were effective and needed no further assistance. Heeding Stark's objections, the Chief Surgeon disbanded the teams.[21]

Another problem with which Fries and his staff had to contend was training in gas defense. When the 1st Division arrived in France, Pershing thought it best to have the Americans train by serving with a French division. This proved to be unsatisfactory because the training varied from unit to unit within the French division. When the Training Section of the AEF's GHQ became operational, it prepared a standardized division training schedule. Initially, the period of time a division spent preparing to enter the line was supposed to be three months.** Only two days of the schedule were allocated to Gas Service instructors. Later, as the demand for combat units increased, the gas instruction decreased to a mere six hours. This was vigorously protested by the Gas Service. In the spring of 1918, when the German offensives required a shortening of the division training cycle to bring new units on line, gas instruction was cut further.[22]

Formal defensive training was supplemented by wearing the masks during other training activities. Pvt. Norman A. Dunham of the 40th Division remembered wearing the SBR and full pack during two- and three-hour marches. He thought the mask "the worst thing a soldier has to contend with" and the "most torturous thing" a person can wear. Lt. Edgar D. Gilman remarked that when he wore the mask he found that it was not only disagreeable, painful, and smothering, but also that his saliva flowed profusely from his mouth, through the flutter valves, and down the front of

---

*Corps hospitals were not considered because a corps was organized exclusively for tactical purposes.

**The 1st Division was retrained at Gondrecourt and was the only AEF Division to complete the AEF's three-month-long training schedule.

56

his shirt. Personal protection was essential for survival on the battlefield, however, and command emphasis had to be placed on defensive gas training, to include the wearing of the mask.[23]

It became obvious to GHQ, AEF that many commanders were not supporting the training activities of their gas officers and NCOs. To remedy this problem, officers in brigades that were rotated off the line received a comprehensive lecture course on gas defensive measures. However, continued reports of over 25 percent gas casualties indicated to the General Staff that, after basic training, comparatively little was to be gained by instructing individuals in units on the line. The consensus among gas officers was that training had to instill an interest and awareness of gas defensive measures throughout an entire unit to give the best results in combat. Gas officers also believed more realistic training was needed. One result of this conviction was that artillery batteries, when they trained, received a minimum of three surprise gas attacks as part of the training schedule. To test the alertness of sentries and to correct such carelessness as leaving masks out of reach, attacks were often scheduled at night, while the troops were sleeping at their position. Men firing on the ranges were subjected to simulated surprise gas attacks in order to familiarize them with laying artillery pieces during an attack and to acquaint them with the difficulty of transmitting firing data while masked. During night marches, men were subjected to gas attacks as a means of teaching them to overcome confusion.

During the first year of American participation in the war, men arriving as individual replacements had little or no formal instruction in defensive measures until they reached their units in the forward areas. In the summer of 1918, the Army acted to rectify this haphazard method. Training stations were established at the AEF debarkation ports of Brest and St.-Nazaire. Each center had five Gas Service instructors: one officer and four NCOs. Three enlisted men acted as gas mask fitters and helpers. When troops arrived at the stations, they marched single file into a warehouse to be fitted and issued masks. After an inspection, the troops moved to a large lecture hall where instructors did everything possible to impress on the men the importance of defensive gas measures. To complete the training, seventy-five to 100 men at a time entered a gas chamber filled with a tear agent for five to ten minutes. At peak times more than 2,000 men a day were put through this initiation into gas warfare.

In Army rear areas, depot divisions,* such as the one at La Querche, handled three categories of personnel: newly arrived line replacements, special units such as engineer troops, and casuals who were recently released from hospitals and scheduled to rejoin their units. During the normal three-week course, the replacements received a minimum of eighteen hours of gas defense training. Their training consisted of lectures, mask drills, games with the mask worn, and firing weapons while wearing the

*The AEF suffered so many casualties that some divisions were broken up, their men used as replacements, and their cadre used to train arriving personnel.

SBR. The troops also went through simulated tactical operations, with the instructors lighting smoke candles and throwing tear gas grenades to provide added realism.

Special troops such as pioneer infantry, engineer, and medical service units first received basic infantry training and then were given three days' intensive instruction in gas defense. During the three days, the men practiced their specialty while wearing masks. For example, medics with SBRs in place applied bandages and carried stretchers through woods and over rough terrain. Engineers constructed roads and pioneer troops dug ditches while wearing masks. After duty hours, trainees played baseball in their SBRs.

Hospital convalescents, the last category of men run through the depot divisions, numbered anywhere from a handful to 2,000 a day. These men were reequipped with masks, and those with prior gas training—Class "A" men—were excused from formal instruction until August, 1918, when the mounting number of mustard gas casualties compelled the Gas Service staff to give all personnel short classes on ways to avoid being contaminated by this persistent agent.

Sanitary Detachment, 121st Machine Gun Battalion, wearing the SBR while playing baseball, 2 June 1918.

58

The increased German employment of chemical agents—especially mustard gas—for counterbattery fire forced American artillery training camps to place special emphasis on defensive gas instruction. During a gas attack, a poorly trained artillery man would be totally incapable of serving his weapon or delivering accurate fire. Initially, artillery officers and NCOs attended a week-long course of lectures, drills, and practical exercises. Later NCOs received an additional week of training. If the artillerymen failed to score 70 percent or better on the final examination, they had to repeat the course. Just before returning to the front, the graduates had to visit a base hospital to see gas casualties. The experience, according to instructors, "furnished a great stimulus to general gas training." Still, despite these efforts to train every doughboy arriving in France, many received no training in gas warfare because of the pressing need for troops on the front lines.[24]

In conjunction with the emphasis on gas defensive training, the AEF paid increasing attention to the offensive gas capabilities of the American Army in France. On 10 January 1918 the first two companies of the 1st Gas Regiment (30th Engineers) arrived in France (Figure 3). The companies reported to the British Special Brigade training area at Helfaut, where Brigadier General Foulkes personally directed the training of the unit. Eventually, four of the six companies of the regiment passed through Helfaut.

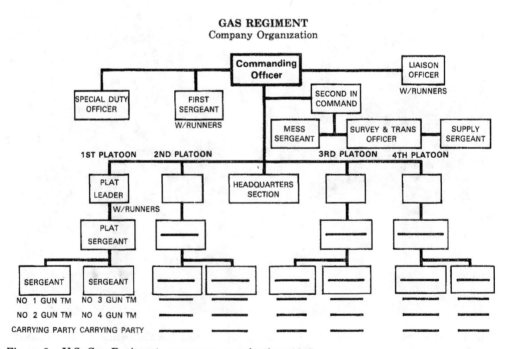

Figure 3. U.S. Gas Regiment, company organization, 1917.

The training of the 1st Gas Regiment in offensive gas operations began in February, 1918, and employed the delivery systems used by the British. The American troops spent five days learning to use Livens projectors, seven days for Stokes mortars, and two days for cylinder operations. The men first attended classes and then conducted practical field exercises in which they applied their newly acquired knowledge. Projector operations called for the emplacement of the guns at night and their detonation the following day. Stokes mortar drill required the men to conduct rapid fire with gas rounds, thermite, and smoke, both day and night. Officers of the regiment opened cylinders of chlorine, and the men walked through the gas cloud to instill confidence in their training and equipment. The American officers were then detailed to a sector of the British front and assigned to Special Brigade companies, where they observed projector, mortar, and cylinder operations. The overall result was that these men better understood offensive gas operations and could assist in training the other companies of the American Gas Regiment.[25]

On 6 June 1918 these trained officers and men held a practice shoot for the AEF General Staff at Hanlon Field, the home of the AEF's Gas School and experimental station in France. Twelve Stokes mortars and 100 Livens projectors were fired. On 22 June, after several more exercises, companies of the 1st Gas Regiment moved to the U.S. sector to conduct offensive gas operations.

Artillery was the other branch of the Army capable of conducting offensive gas operations. In the first gas warfare manuals prepared by the U.S. Army War College, artillery employment was not included because of the continual changes in gas tactical doctrine* on the Western Front. Therefore, almost all artillery training in gas warfare was conducted in France, where the AEF adopted British and French doctrine for gas shell fire. The U.S. 1st Army, for example, published its own "Provisional Instruction for Artillery Officers on the Use of Gas Shell," based on French field manuals. At artillery camps, gas officers lectured on the problems involved in the use of gas shells, but no evidence exists to indicate that gas shells were ever fired in training. Yet, by 1 November 1918, 20 percent of all shells delivered to the AEF were gas filled, and a 25 percent ratio was planned for 1919.[26]

No other preparations or plans were instituted in AEF rear areas to prepare and sustain the American armies in chemical warfare. The burden of the gas war fell to the combat divisions of the AEF. How well they fought and how well they adapted to this new experience is the subject of the next chapter.

---

*Firing with gas shells was such a new experience that the opposing armies changed their doctrine on a regular basis seeking the most effective means of employment.

"The Quick and the Dead":
The AEF on the
Chemical Battlefield

Between 18 and 21 January 1918, units of the U.S. 1st Infantry Division relieved the French 1st Moroccan Division manning the front lines in the Ansauville sector. In doing so, the "Big Red One" became the first American division to occupy a portion of the Western Front. The movement of American troops into the lines was uneventful except for one incident. "As we take our positions in the trenches," Maj. Gen. Robert Bullard, the division commander, noted, "from the French position on our right some two hundred gas casualties are evacuated—our first object lesson."[1]

This grim "object lesson" reinforced French warnings that the Ansauville sector was a highly active gas front with both sides constantly employing large amounts of chemical agents. The German use of Yellow Cross especially concerned the French. The XXII Corps commander, prior to the arrival of the 1st Division, had his troops post in every dugout instructions in English on the correct procedures to follow during and after a Yellow Cross attack. The French warning advised the Americans to mask when the first gas shell exploded and remain masked for four hours following a gas bombardment. The instructions also called for anyone in a gassed area to beat and shake his clothing prior to entering a dugout and to use soapy water to decontaminate skin exposed to mustard. Further instructions from the French corps commander followed, emphasizing the gas-proofing of dugouts and the maintenance of gas mask discipline.[2]

Based on the 1st Division's experience over the previous months, these instructions should not have been necessary. Although the unit arrived overseas without the slightest bit of gas training, it received in France the most complete chemical warfare preparation of any AEF division during the war. Gas training pamphlets, directives, and orders were showered on the 1st Division by an anxious and apprehensive GHQ, AEF. The 1st Division became the only American division to undergo the complete GHQ, AEF, training schedule, which included defensive and offensive gas training.*

*Even with this extensive training, the mistakes made by the soldiers of this division during chemical warfare were the very same repeated over and over by other, less prepared AEF divisions. In the Ansauville and the Montdidier sectors, the Big Red One suffered more casualties from gas than from small arms or artillery shell fire.

"Big Nims," 366th Infantry, 92nd Division, inspecting his mask (note mouthpiece), 8 August 1918.

Instruction in chemical warfare began for the 1st Division in December with nine hours devoted to defensive training. Proper masking was a key element of this training. With troops in the practice trenches, instructors sounded gas alarms and lit smoke pots to simulate gas clouds, thereby increasing the troops' "skill in putting on and wearing the gas masks." During the drill, gas instructors reminded their students that "in case of gas attack, there are only two classes of soldiers, the quick and the dead."[3]

The British had decided for reasons now obscure that SBR masking should take no longer than six seconds, to be accomplished in five steps. In step one, the doughboy had to hold his breath,* knock off his headgear, grip his rifle between the legs, and reach into the case on his chest to grasp the mask by the "breathing joint" and nose clip. At step two, the soldier thrust his chin out, held the mask in front of the face with both thumbs inside and under the elastic head band. In step three, the chin was

*Officers realized that, when exposed to German gas in combat, men instinctively took a deep breath. In so doing, they unintentionally inhaled the poisonous air. Later, the AEF corrected the drill by instructing the doughboy to "stop breathing" when the gas alarm sounded.

placed into the facepiece while the headband was pulled over the head to secure the mask. Next, at step four, the soldier grasped the mouthpiece with his teeth. The last step, five, required the soldier to reach through the facepiece to secure the nose clip and then run his hands around the mask to ensure a snug fit. Division gas officers complained that when it came to defensive gas training, many commanders were satisfied when their men simply achieved the six-second requirement. Proper adjustment, the gas officers believed, was more important than speed.[4]

When finally issued, each mask came with a small log book tied to the canvas case. Soldiers received instructions to record the length of time they wore the mask, both for drill and in combat. They were also required to identify each type of gas encountered. The purpose of this log was to ensure that the filter in the canister was replaced at the proper interval. Filters for an SBR had a life of fifty to 100 hours of exposure, depending on the chemical agents. As might be expected, the log system did not work. As one gas officer remarked, "any man who in the hell of battle can keep such a record completely should be at once awarded a Distinguished Service Medal." Gas officers in some divisions came up with an alternative: they painted the number of the month of issue on the case. If and when filters became available, the officers replaced them based on their own estimate of exposure time. There were three types of AEF filter canisters. Those

Men of the 366th Infantry, 92nd Division, during an inspection of their American SBRs at Ainville, Vosges, France, 8 August 1918.

painted black were for training only and offered no protection against smoke or gas. Canisters colored yellow protected against smoke, offered greater gas protection, and had a high resistance to breathing. The green canister offered protection against smoke, had "sufficient" gas protection, and had a low resistance to breathing.[5]

While the British SBR was initially worn by the 1st and other divisions, the American version was in ready supply by the late summer of 1918. The

Medics place an M-2 mask on a head-wound casualty, 137th Ambulance Company, 31 August 1918.

American mask had both advantages and disadvantages. Although its fuller facepiece permitted easy cleaning of the eyepieces, these eyepieces had a tendency to fall out; also, the larger facepiece with an increase in dead space made it more difficult to clear. The larger canister gave greater protection, but was heavier and clumsy.[6]

There is no question but that the SBR, whether British or American, was extremely uncomfortable. General Bullard admitted that he could never "fulfill the qualification of a successful wearer" because as much as he tried he could not wear the mask longer than three minutes without feeling smothered. Since the SBR was difficult to wear, division gas officers reported troops would change from the SBR to the more comfortable M-2 in the midst of a gas attack, in the process inhaling the poisonous air. The M-2 did not offer the filtration protection of the SBR. Its flimsy construction and susceptibility to water damage also reduced its effectiveness, as did the fact that it did not block mustard gas. The widespread problem with the M-2 prompted AEF, GHQ General Order 78 on 25 May 1918. This order forbid anyone who entered the alert zone* to use the M-2. As noted previously it was retained and attached to stretchers for men with head wounds or for those unable to grasp the mouthpiece. Labor troops in rear areas were authorized to wear the M-2.[7]

A number of U.S. officers apparently procured, on their own, another French mask, the ARS (described earlier). This created morale problems since it gave American enlisted men the "impression that our protective equipment is defective." A Gas Service report demanded that these officers "be taught" that only the material issued by the Gas Service was authorized for use, and that they had no authority to secure equipment from the French.[8]

Another mask, the *Tissot*, was officially procured from the French, although it was for issue only in "small numbers" to artillerymen, Signal Corps troops, and front-line medical units whose personnel had to be active during gas attacks. Not only did this mask's filter offer less resistance to breathing and have the same quality filtration of the American SBR, but the problem of fogged vision associated with the SBR did not exist. The *Tissot* design allowed air to flow between the two lenses of each eyepiece, eliminating condensation. Most important, the *Tissot* design did away with a nose clip and mouthpiece, making it a comfortable yet safe mask.[9] Unfortunately, as noted earlier, the filter location on the back, together with the flimsy rubber facepiece, made it unsuitable for infantry.

If soldiers wearing gas masks in defensive positions experienced a variety of problems, they encountered even more difficulties when they shifted to the offensive. The standard issue American or British SBR made *normal* breathing difficult; it made obtaining sufficient oxygen during heavy exertion, such as in infantry attacks across No Man's Land, impossible. Additionally,

---

*"Standing Orders for Defense Against Gas" published in November, 1917, stated that within two miles of the front lines and within areas specially exposed to gas shelling, the gas mask case would be carried in the alert position, which was on the chest.

Lt. William T. Powers, Pvt. Walter Miesley, Operator, and Pvt. Richard Pereyer, Recorder, wearing the *Tissot* mask while receiving instructions from a forward observer, 30 October 1918.

exertion caused perspiration to form on the lens, limiting vision even more than what was normal.*

At Ville Savoye, for example, Pvt. Moses King, 305th Infantry, 77th Division, had difficulty seeing through his mask and received an order from his company commander—whose own vision was obscured—to remove his facepiece, but to keep the nose clip and mouthpiece in place. This "pernicious habit," the Chief, Chemical Warfare Service, AEF, noted in September 1918, "has been the cause of many casualties"; the practice has been "condemned at every opportunity." Despite the condemnation, the practice never ceased, and the increased use of mustard gas by the Germans resulted in a significant number of Allied casualties suffering from eye damage.[10]

As a consequence of these and other problems, standing orders did not call for troops to mask during the attack. Doughboys did, however, wear the mask on the chest in the alert position with the helmet chin strap on the tip of the chin, rather than under it, to facilitate quick placement of the mask if gas were encountered.[11]

---

*"Anti-dimming" (defogging) paste was issued with the mask, but according to soldiers who used it, it distorted the vision of the mask wearer.

In addition to the problems associated with gas masks, the persistency of chemical agents combined with the methods of AEF commanders to produce a significant number of gas casualties. Under normal attacking conditions, an area in which phosgene was used would clear in ten minutes. Diphosgene would take longer to dispel, perhaps fifteen to twenty minutes. Mustard gas would linger for several days. A problem arose, however, when AEF commanders intent on taking an objective regardless of the cost often launched an attack before a gassed area had cleared. The reason for this disregard lay in the fact that the AEF, from General Pershing down to division commanders, never hesitated to relieve an officer considered lacking in an aggressive spirit.

Of the chemical agents employed by the Germans against the Allies, mustard gas was responsible for 39 percent of AEF gas casualties. Once mustard gas made contact with the skin, it destroyed tissue as long as it remained, doing damage several hours before the first symptoms appeared. To combat this persistent blister agent, the Gas Service made available to line units an ointment called Sag paste* to protect exposed flesh. Sag paste came in a 3.5-cm by 16-cm collapsible tube and became a standard-issue item for the prevention and treatment of mustard burns. According to one veteran, it looked like and had the consistency of "carbolated vaseline." Doughboys who entered a mustard-contaminated area or who anticipated a shelling of Yellow Cross smeared their bodies with the ointment. It proved very effective, a medic in the 35th Division noted, if used in time. However, it was uncomfortable because it caked when the men perspired and rubbed off on clothing when a soldier engaged in any physical activity. The paste also presented a danger: if not removed after exposure to gas it eventually absorbed the mustard agent without neutralizing it, which meant that the agent ultimately came into contact with the skin. There were other uses for the paste: medics, for example, found it to be effective in soothing mustard burns by blocking the oxygen to the contaminated area. Enterprising men in the trenches found it extremely effective in exterminating "cooties," the doughboy slang for body lice.[12]

The Defense Division, CWS, sought other ways besides masks and Sag paste to protect troops from mustard gas. The division designed and had manufactured a protective suit for artillery gun crews, medics, and decontaminating teams. The suit consisted of cotton sheeting impregnated with linseed or "vegetable drying oil." The coveralls had elastic ties at the ankles and wrists. A zipper down the center from neck to crotch provided an airtight fit. The hood was worn under the headgear. Mittens had been provided prior to the development of the suit and were "highly valuable . . . but somewhat stiff and clumsy."** Special boots were also provided to complete the uniform. Unfortunately, the suit trapped body heat and moisture so it could rarely be worn longer than fifteen to thirty minutes. A gas officer

*I was unable to identify the source of the term "Sag." Lt. Col. Charles M. Wurm, CACDA, Ft. Leavenworth, suggested "Salve, Antigas."

**Gloves were not available until the end of the war.

68

reported men tearing off the suit "while working in an area reeking with mustard gas because they couldn't stand the discomfort any longer."[13]

The effects of mustard gas could be lessened or even avoided by removing it with hot soapy water shortly after exposure. To this end, GHQ, AEF, on 29 August 1918, ordered the Medical Department to activate a number of

Pvt. John Sloan, 6th Infantry Medical Detachment, in an "Anti-Gas Suit," Croix de Charemont, France, 20 August 1918. This protective uniform was worn by medical personnel and artillery gun crews.

"Degassing Station" tank truck with heater mounted in the rear, Mobile Degassing Unit #1, Services of Supply, Tours, France, 21 July 1918.

"mobile degassing units." Each division in the "line of battle" would have two such units attached, commanded by a Sanitary Corps captain or first lieutenant. To each eleven-man unit a specially trained medical gas officer would be detailed from the supported division. This individual's duties included the supervision of the unit's operation, instruction of the medical personnel on the treatment of gas casualties, and responsibility for the maintenance of the proper equipment for the treatment of gas casualties at the battalion advance aid station. The degassing units remained in the division rear. When a unit became contaminated and could be withdrawn from the line, the degassing station rushed to treat the men as close to the front as possible. The unit's equipment consisted of a five-ton tank truck with a 1,200 gallon capacity and an "instantaneous heater" mounted on the rear of the vehicle to provide hot water. The heated water flowed to portable shower baths similar to modern field showers. Another vehicle carried fuel, underwear, uniforms, and medical supplies. These supplies included bicarbonate of soda to flush the patient's eyes, ears, mouth, and nasal passages. Unfortunately for the thousands of mustard casualties, very few degassing units saw service, as evidenced by the late date of the order creating them.*[14]

*When the Armistice took effect, the few units that had reached the field were turned over to the Quartermaster Corps for delousing troops returning home.

While methods were being sought to "degas" men, efforts were also undertaken to decontaminate the ground they held in the static trench warfare. General orders created decontamination squads at regiment and battalion level. These units decontaminated shell holes with lime and new earth, buried gas shell duds, reported to gas officers the location of dud shells that could not be buried, and removed contaminated equipment and clothing in special oiled bags. Each man in the squad was issued a new SBR, a reserve M-2 mask, a suit of protective coveralls, and two pairs of oiled mittens. The decontamination equipment consisted of shovels, buckets, and long-handled tongs for handling dud mustard shells.

In the trenches, mustard gas and other agents were counteracted in a variety of ways. During a gas attack, standing orders called for as little moving about and talking as possible, because gas poisoning was sometimes intensified by exertion. Once an attack ceased, trenches were cleared of low lying gas. One method required the use of an Ayrton or trench fan. This device consisted of a two-foot-long handle attached to a rigid piece of canvas hinged to a fifteen-inch section that moved in one direction. In effect the fan was used like a shovel, with the moveable flap creating an upward air current, thus removing the gas. Americans adopted these fans as called for

A squad preparing to decontaminate a gas shell hole, 4 December 1918.

Men detailed to use Ayrton or British trench fans after gas attack, 1918.

by British defensive gas doctrine. Unfortunately, the fans, according to British General Foulkes, were "worse than worthless." Not only did they not remove the vapor, but the exertion of masked users led to exhaustion and increased susceptibility to gassing.* The fans were eventually discarded and burned to create an updraft, soon recognized as a better method of clearing trenches and dugouts of gas.[15]

Another method of decontamination used in the trenches consisted of placing boxes of chloride of lime outside of dugouts. Prior to entering, men stepped in the substance, neutralizing any mustard agent clinging to the shoes. The Vermoral sprayer, which was a hand-pumped fire extinguisher filled with a sodium thiosulfate solution, could neutralize chlorine, but little else. The sprayers were used, however, to moisten the blankets at the entrances of the gas-proof dugouts.[16]

The prolongation of German gas attacks, the increased quantity of chemical agents fired in an attack, the extensive use of the persistent agent mustard, plus the fact that 80 percent to 90 percent of all gas attacks experienced by the AEF took place during the hours of darkness, made the construction of gas-proof dugouts essential for survival in the trenches (Figure 4). Basically, the gas-proofing of dugouts required a wood frame entrance and a snug fitting blanket, usually soaked with glycerine and kept damp

*Apparently the British Army first rejected the fan, an invention of Mrs. Ayrton, the wife of a distinguished physicist, but political pressure forced them to procure 100,000. The AEF Gas Service, unaware of the circumstances and not thinking to ask, ordered 50,000.

with a diluted solution of sodium thiosulfate. If space allowed, "complete protection" could be obtained by hanging two blankets over the entrance in such a way as to leave an air space between the two. Such measures made it difficult for men in front-line trenches to get out of a dugout rapidly in the event of an infantry attack, and for this reason early U.S. manuals advised against protection of front-line dugouts. But this advice was generally ignored because of the need to have a gas-free environment in which to sleep and occasionally remove the SBR. The same Army manual stated that "Medical aid-posts and advanced dressing stations; Company, Regiment, and Brigade Headquarters; at least one dugout per battery position; Signal Shelters and any other place where work has to be carried out during a gas attack should *always* be protected."[17]

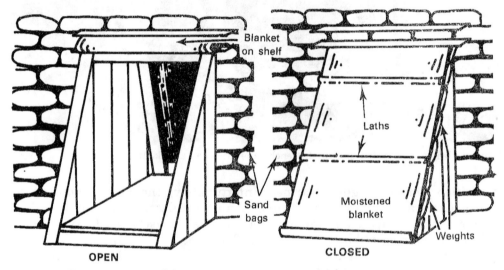

Figure 4. Entrance, gas-proof dugout

Oftentimes, casualties occurred when a gas shell or projector shell fell at the entrance of a dugout and the force of the explosion threw open the blankets and drove the gas inside. On 27 May 1918, at the beginning of one of the German 1918 spring offensives, a concentration of 983 phosgene projector bombs caught doughboys of the 168th Infantry, 42nd Division, asleep in dugouts on the side of a ravine. The Germans, in order to keep the U.S. troops pinned in the gassed position, shelled the area in the rear of the ravine for an hour with shrapnel and Yellow Cross. The division G-3 reported one soldier killed and six wounded by shrapnel, 236 gassed, and thirty-seven gas deaths resulting from the attack.[18]

It was the duty of the gas sentry to sound the warning of a gas attack to the other troops. Usually the sentry received general instructions to alert his unit as soon as he heard the hissing sound of gas leaving cylinders, saw a cloud moving along the ground, observed a distant flash, heard a muffled explosion of projectors, saw a shell burst with a small pop, or sniffed a suspicious odor. In addition to shouting, "Gas!" he would, after masking, sound a mechanical alarm. Such alarms ranged from air horns, known as

Pvt Demetry Melonisk, 315th Field Hospital, 304th Sanitary Train, 79th Division, carrying a church bell used to give gas alarms, 17 October 1918.

Strombos,* to metal shell casings, steel triangles, or even church bells. When, in the fall of 1918, the AEF went on the offensive, the Gas Service decided that Klaxon horns and European police rattles produced the most audible warning of gas to troops on the move.[19]

*Strombos horns carried for a great distance and were initially used for cloud attacks that occurred over a wide frontage. Later in the war, when attacks became more localized with projectiles and shells, the Strombos were phased out and replaced with alarms whose sound did not carry as far.

Whether on the move in open warfare or manning the trenches in static warfare, the most critical individuals in chemical combat were the unit gas officers. On 27 May 1918, AEF General Order 79 formalized and standardized defensive duties for gas officers, the positions having been created by individual divisions on their own initiative after arrival in France. Two months later, General Order 107 expanded the functions of gas officers: in addition to their previous duties, they would be advisers whose technical knowledge would be solicited "in the preparations of all plans involving the extensive use of gas, whether by artillery or by other means." Despite the order, staff officers too often told gas officers that their advice for offensive planning was not required and that they should concern themselves only with defensive duties. The success of division gas officers in integrating plans for the use of gas in offensive operations eventually depended on, in the words of the Gas Service's Chief, their ability to "go out and sell gas to the army." Despite such promotional efforts, resistance by staff officers continued. During the Meuse-Argonne campaign in the fall of 1918, an unidentified division gas officer reportedly recommended to a division operations officer (G-3) that gas be used during a particular phase of the engagement. The staff officer replied that he would employ the artillery firing gas shells only if the gas officer stated in writing that the gas would not cause a single American casualty. This request was unrealistic in that a thorough staff planner in World War I "usually included an allowance for casualties due to a friendly barrage."* Another objection raised to the use of gas was that commanders feared its employment would subject their men to unnecessary retaliatory gas attacks.[20]

Even if a division commander and his staff were reluctant to employ chemicals, they could not afford to be careless about the protection of their troops from chemical agents. A unit's effectiveness depended on proper gas defensive measures. GHQ, AEF, delegated significant responsibility for gas defense to division, regiment, battalion, and company gas officers and NCOs. These dedicated and harried men attempted to insure that their respective organizations could cope with gas attacks while sustaining minimal casualties. Once in the trenches, exposed to a chemical warfare environment, most commanders soon realized the need for competent gas officers. After selection and training, gas officers had to prove themselves to the commander, staff, and the troops in the trenches. The most effective way to gain the respect and confidence of the troops, one gas officer discovered, was to join a unit under an attack. This practice offered a number of advantages. First, the gas officer learned the immediate effects of a gas attack and what individuals endured during such an attack. He could suggest corrections and give guidance during the attack, as opposed to afterwards, when men were already casualties. The confidence of the men in the gas officer's instruction grew when they observed him "take what they did." Infantry officers proved more willing to accept the advice of such a gas officer because they knew he spoke from "actual and not book knowledge."

*No figures for the AEF are available, but the French concluded that 75,000 or 1.5 percent of all their casualties were due to amicicide (casualties caused by friendly fire).

This knowledge afforded the gas officer the credibility to obtain a "hearing and accomplish results" when he called to the attention of unit officers and staff both "good results of proper gas discipline and the bad results of bad discipline."[21]

While division gas officers worked with the staff, the regimental and battalion gas officers had the greatest impact on the doughboys. At these lower echelons, gas officers assumed a variety of responsibilities that ranged from instruction to inspection of defensive equipment and selection of alternate positions during an attack. It fell to these officers to assure that gas alarms were installed, gas sentries posted, gas alert signs displayed, and dugouts selected for gas-proofing. In addition these officers took wind readings twice a day.* When required, gas officers became bomb disposal experts who located and removed all unexploded enemy gas shells. As the Table of Organization for AEF units did not include gas officers, General Order 79 of 27 May 1918, which ordered the appointment of gas officers down to battalion level, caused some grumbling in recently arrived divisions. Plagued by a shortage of line officers, commanders assigned men to gas duties grudgingly. When the need arose, the men chosen were subjected to double duty as infantry officers.[22]

With the absence of sophisticated detection and warning systems, one of the most important functions of a gas officer became the determination of when to give the order to mask and when to unmask. At gas schools, trainees were taught to "taste" gas, sniffing just enough air to identify a chemical agent by its own peculiar odor. They had to know the persistency and the properties of each gas and then be able to determine how soon after an attack the air would clear. Most of the officers became very proficient at identification. At times, though, some gas officers were "too conscientious" in "tasting" for gas and became casualties themselves.[23]

When night settled in, gas officers in the trenches slept fitfully, waiting for the cry of "Gas!" One such officer described an evening that was shattered, after the troops had gone to sleep, by the sound of artillery followed by gas alarms. Everyone, he recalled, "came out of their holes" with masks in place, the "fine fruit" of constant training. The officer lifted his mask, sniffed, and determined the fumes to be from high explosive shells. After taking his mask off, the gas officer gave the all clear and the men unmasked. Toward dawn the men again awoke to the sound of gas alarms and cries of "Gas!" This time the officer raised his mask and detected the "mild pungent breath" of a chemical agent. He masked and told the others to do the same. A gas shell exploded upwind with a "light pop and puff of vapor." After the shells ceased dropping he checked up and down the line for casualties and found none. Several minutes passed, and he took another taste only to detect a lingering odor. Five minutes later a light wind drove the gas away, and the all-clear sounded.[24]

*Early in the American involvement, AEF and War Department manuals listed cloud attacks as the primary delivery system of the Germans; when the wind blew from the east, therefore, troops went on a gas alert.

The Americans were not always so fortunate in responding to gas attacks. On 26 February 1918, at 1330 in the Ansauville sector, men of the 1st Division received the first German projector attack directed against U.S. forces. The estimated 150 to 250 bombs contained phosgene and chloropicrin. Conditions were ideal for such an attack: the heavy evening air kept the gas low to the ground, and what wind there was soon became calm. The bombs fell over a 600-meter front, where heavy underbrush held the gas in place. Of the 225 men exposed, 33 percent (eighty-five men) became casualties. Two men died soon after the attack, and six soldiers succumbed after they reached the division field hospital.

Col. Campbell King, 1st Division Chief of Staff, believed that there were several causes for the casualties. The sudden attack caught men unprepared on sentry duty or in their dugouts; they did not have adequate warning to adjust their masks or lower the gas curtains. After the attack, men removed their masks on their own initiative, or changed to the M-2, although the gas lingered in a dangerous concentration. Furthermore, the unmasked doughboys remained or worked in the dugouts and in low places in the woods, where gas stagnated. A captain who witnessed the attack amplified the Chief of Staff's observation. He reiterated that the premature removal of the mask, a breach of discipline, caused casualties and that the men failed to mask in time and to lower the gas-proof curtains. At the same time, the soldiers neglected to put out fires in the dugouts, thereby drawing gas from the trenches into the sealed shelters. Men who were only slightly gassed exerted themselves, contrary to standing orders, thus complicating their symptoms. The captain attributed the donning of the M-2 to the discomfort involved in wearing the SBR. A field hospital report mentioned that one man had had his mask disarranged in an attempt to force a mask on a comrade who had gone berserk and torn off his own mask.[25]

In another commonplace incident, an entire platoon of infantry in the 28th Division became gas casualties before they reached the front. While moving forward one night toward Châuteau Thierry, the men stopped to rest in shallow shell holes near the road. A recent rain had diluted the usual smell of mustard, and no one advised the green troops that the holes were craters from Yellow Cross shells. Unwittingly, they slept through the night in fresh mustard contamination. The following morning the men awoke with backs and buttocks so badly burned that the skin appeared to be flayed. The battalion gas officer could only try to relieve their agony with generous applications of Sag paste. That same day the 28th Division's gas officer noted his dwindling supplies of paste and masks. Since German gas seemed to be "coming over in increasing quantities with the resulting casualties," he ordered one of the battalion gas officers back to the SOS depot at Gievres on a foraging expedition to secure antigas supplies for the division.[26]

There were times when division, regimental, and battalion gas officers, in their more zealous attempts to prevent gas casualties, ran afoul of line officers. A battalion commander in the 23d Infantry, 2d Division, complained to his superior that the requests, orders, and reports required by the regimental gas officer were "absurd, ludicrous, and, in many cases, impossible" to carry out. For instance, the gas officer had ordered that all men within 1,200 yards of the front line must sleep in gas-proof dugouts with a sentry posted over each. If this order were respected, the commander complained, no one in the unit would get any rest because the facilities for compliance did not exist. Another directive informed the infantry officer that men exposed to mustard should take a warm bath and change uniforms. To this he replied, with frustration, "We don't get enough water to wash regularly." The battalion commander closed his letter by explaining how tired he was of receiving directives "doped out of a book." Staff officers, he believed, must become more aware of the conditions at the front.[27]

Infantrymen of the 28th Division masking during a gas attack, 23 August 1918.

Likewise a division commander complained that new gas officers were "almost hysterical" in their attempts to educate the troops in gas defense. "Knowledge and real efficient training," he observed, "came after hard experience" and the "hysteria" of gas officers passed. When the 1st Division suffered 800 gas casualties at Villers-Tournelle, General Bullard complained of a report filed by a GHQ gas officer who, he believed, "spoke without knowledge or consideration" in a tone of "superior criticism" that comes from "abstract study." After Bullard complained, the officer's superiors ordered all gas officers to abstain from such criticism. Fortunately, incidents such as these were the exception rather than the rule, and line officers eventually realized that the gas officers were there to help them, not to harass them.[28]

Still, the job of gas officer continued to be a demanding one, especially in regard to defensive training for replacements. The "square"* World War I division had a Table of Organization strength of approximately 28,000 officers and men. In this war of attrition with high casualties (referred to as "wastage"), these large square divisions had a constant flow of new men into the ranks. The 1st Division, for example, after 223 days in the line, received over 30,000 replacements. The 2nd Division's statistics were even more striking: following 139 days in the trenches, it took in over 35,000 new men. Six other divisions received over half their strength in replacements, and another five received over a third. The rapid mobilization and rush to send men overseas led to a situation in which men had little overall training. The 42nd Division, after some time in the trenches, withdrew to train for the St. Mihiel offensive. During this time the division received replacements, "cannon fodder if there ever was any." One company obtained forty-three new men of whom "one man had had but one week of training; four had had two weeks; twenty had had three weeks; six had had four weeks"; and the balance had had between one and three months. Gas officers were therefore faced with a continual personnel training problem, having to instill a proper respect for gas defense in green officers and men.[29]

Protecting officers and men of the AEF required more than training. Contamination of food, water, tobacco, and equipment by chemical agents emerged as a significant problem for gas officers. On an interim basis the Gas Service issued tar paper and oil cloth to cover food and tobacco. Water contamination was always a problem, because the scarcity of water often compelled men like a 79th Division doughboy at Montfaucon to risk drinking from a suspicious source. Driven by thirst, this American ignored the warning of French soldiers and drank stagnant water from a shell hole. He later suffered chest pains from the gas contaminated water. After being evacuated he eventually returned to his unit, but only after twenty-three days in a base hospital. No one ever devised an effective means to stop troops from drinking contaminated water. Late in the war, the Quartermaster Corps packaged foodstuffs destined for France in gas-proof, airtight trench ration containers.

As for equipment, the corrosive properties of most war gases created problems of contaminated artillery shells not being able to be chambered, breechblocks jamming, gun surfaces rusting, and contaminated small arms cartridges not chambering properly. AEF regulations required weapons and shells be cleaned with oil immediately after a gas attack, but the metal continued to corrode unless small arms were disassembled and boiled in a solution of sodium bicarbonate and water. The difficulty of applying this decontamination method in the trenches, not to mention in No Man's Land during a prolonged assault lasting several days, can be well imagined. Protection of animals was also a problem, and they, too, were fitted with protective masks.[30]

When doughboys went "over the top," they, their commanders, and their gas officers alike faced increased challenges and "many difficulties not met

*The term "square" comes from the fact that the division had four infantry regiments.

The use of chemical agents created problems not only for the combat arms but also for the Services of Supply, the logistical tail of the AEF. Here mules and men are masked for a drill, November, 1918.

with in trench warfare." At times, good gas discipline had little or no impact on casualties in the maelstrom of battle. The reports of gas officers constantly referred to gas casualties caused by men being "knocked down, or shocked and stunned" by German high explosive shell fire. The concussion of the exploding shells slowed the men's reaction or worse, knocked them unconscious, and they never had a chance to put their mask on. Many times the blast tore off a mask or flying shrapnel cut the facepiece or damaged the hose from the filter to the mouthpiece. The extensive use of gas both at day and night often meant prolonged use of the mask. Lt. Robert A. Hall, for example, blamed a significant number of the 1st Division's gas casualties at Villers-Tournelle on the fact that after seventeen to eighteen hours of good gas discipline wearing the SBR, perspiration impregnated with gas seeped under the elastic head band. Perspiration also caused the nose clip to slip, and as a result, men inhaled poisonous vapor or had their eyes affected and, as a consequence, became gas casualties.[31]

Troops caught in the open by enemy gunners often sought cover in shell holes, ravines, and patches of wood, the very places where gas lingered the longest. Even if men maintained strict gas discipline, casualties were inevitable when the enemy concentration of gas shells became too dense. From 0600, 12 October, to 1600, 13 October 1918, the 114th Infantry, 29th Division, attacked German positions at Bois Ormout. The Germans fired an estimated 2,000 gas shells at the regiment in bursts of about 300. Yellow, Green, and Blue Cross 77-mm and 105-mm shells landed around the 1,500 men of the 114th Infantry while they deployed in ravines, shell holes, and wooded areas. As a consequence, 500 men became gas casualties, mostly with lung injuries. The commander requested permission to evacuate the contaminated area. The French 66th Regiment commander, who had operational control of the attack, told him to remain in place. The Frenchman believed the withdrawal of the regiment was not tactically sound, for the Germans would counterattack if they detected any sign of an Allied retreat. Maj. James H. Walton, the division gas officer, remarked that this incident, in which high gas casualties were inflicted despite good gas discipline, was one of the "best examples of the deadly effects of gas shell" he had seen in combat.[32]

Combat decisions that had little reference to gas warfare often resulted in incurring or aggravating gas casualties. For example, although AEF tactical doctrine called for the preselection of alternate positions, many requests to relocate infantry units during combat were denied even though the tactical situation and the enemy's use of chemical agents called for relocation. In the determination to show the AEF's battle prowess, many of its senior commanders were loath to give up an inch of occupied or captured ground. In one such case, on 15 July 1918, the commander of the 30th Infantry, 3d Division, filed a graphic report of the unit's plight after repelling a German attempt to cross the Marne. His men, after being shelled with various chemicals for ten hours, were "absolutely worn out." They had not had "even a drink of water" during that time. The shells landing in their sector contained mustard, chloropicrin, and "chocolate" (diphosgene has the odor of candy) gases. If the men remained in their contaminated uniforms, he noted, they were certain to become gas casualties, because the mustard gas would eventually reach their flesh. It was "absolutely impossible" to feed the regiment because the rations had been contaminated by the gas. He reported to division that "they are still there in the line and they will hold the line, but they ought to be relieved. . . ." They were not.* Such decisions exhibited a crucial lack of understanding of the nature of gas warfare.[33]

Like the infantry, AEF artillerymen and animals suffered under the fury of German gas shell bombardments. While nonpersistent gas caused artillerymen problems in their attempt to deliver accurate fire, "mustard-yellow cross gas," remarked a cannoneer with the 91st Division, "seems to be about the only Boche weapon of which the men are really afraid." Efforts were made to displace batteries subjected to counterbattery gas attacks, but this was difficult and time consuming. To assist the artillerymen who had to remain in a gassed area, the French *Tissot* mask was issued when available. As previously noted, not only did this mask's filter offer less resistance to breathing, but the problem of fogged vision associated with the SBR did not exist. Most important, without a nose clip and mouthpiece it was a very comfortable mask to wear. In addition to the *Tissot* mask, gas gloves made of oil cloth were issued together with "impervious clothing." However, because the antigas suits were not ventilated, men would tear them off in warm weather even while working in an area reeking with

*Gas casualties for the 30th Infantry during the period 14—20 July 1918 totaled 202 out of a total of 600 for the 3rd Division. (Spencer, *Gas Attacks*, Part 1, p. 123.)

mustard. As an alternative to the protective coveralls, artillerymen used Sag paste. Many artillerymen shaved off all their body hair prior to an application of the ointment. "Every man in the firing battery," noted a gunner, "is now denuded of hair on top of his poll, under his arm pits, between his legs, and his underwear is soldered to him with 'sag paste.' "[34]

A horse and cannoneer masked during a gas attack, 1918.

Battery A, 108th Field Artillery, receiving and firing gas counterbattery fire, 3 October 1918.

The German use of chemical agents during World War I also placed a tremendous burden on a noncombat branch, the AEF Medical Department. Initially, no actions were taken at division level to provide medics with special expertise in the treatment of chemical casualties. As a result, division medical personnel were unprepared initially to handle the influx of gas victims. In the confusion of organizing and placing an American army in combat, it took GHQ, AEF, until October, 1918, to establish a uniform procedure to handle casualties.

The 42d Division, the second most experienced American combat division of the AEF, appointed a gas medical officer—a position that eventually all divisions of the AEF were ordered to establish. The 42d's decision to appoint a gas medical officer came in the wake of several disastrous contacts with chemical agents in the division's early combat. One such incident occurred on the evening of 20 March 1917, when approximately 400 German mustard rounds and 7,000 high explosive and shrapnel shells landed on a position manned by the division's 165th Infantry. The weather conditions were excellent for the persistent mustard agent. It had rained earlier, and there was no breeze to dissipate the gas as it hung in the air. At midnight, men began to suffer the delayed effects of the gas. Company K lost two-thirds of its effectives. A week later Lt. Col. H. L. Gilchrist, Medical Director of the AEF, reported observing at a base hospital 417 gas casualties from the 165th Infantry.[35]

As the intensity of fighting increased, so did the number of men who claimed they were gassed, further burdening the Medical Department. Many shell-shocked soldiers or men who suffered from exhaustion and hunger believed themselves to be victims of gas poisoning. Others panicked after smelling shell fumes and reported themselves gassed. Then there were the shirkers who feigned being gassed. "The symptomology of gas poisoning is so complex," observed Maj. William V. Sommervell, 3d Division Gas Officer, "and at the same time so indefinite" that anyone who claimed to be gassed was immediately sent to the rear.[36]

As a consequence GHQ, AEF, expanded the number of medical personnel available to diagnose gas victims and weed out malingerers. At the hospital to the rear, division medical personnel devised several traps to detect suspected malingerers. One trap involved offering the gas casualty a large meal. Men on the front line were always hungry; they rarely had enough to eat. But a gas victim's symptoms would include a loss of appetite, so anyone who devoured the food found himself promptly returned to the line. Medical personnel also offered suspected malingerers a cigarette laced with diphosgene. If the soldier gagged he was feigning gas poisoning. Some idea of the magnitude of the problem may be derived from one division field hospital commander's establishment of a board to review the 251 gas cases

Lts. Lautell Lugar and William A. Howell, Medical Corps, attending wounded to the rear of the first trench line during a gas attack, 27 October 1918.

in his wards. The board's report indicated that only ninety of the men actually suffered from gas poisoning. The problem, though, was never satisfactorily resolved in the AEF.[37]

The Medical Department processed gas casualties in combat divisions, using procedures similar to those used for sick and wounded. Medics at the battalion aid stations did what they could for the gas wounded. This consisted of plastering Sag paste on mustard burns, often having to cut a uniform open to expose the swollen flesh. A wet compress applied over the eyes eased the pain of those blinded. Men who inhaled mustard gas could only be comforted with words, for no treatment could ease their pain. Medics could do nothing "but try to put [the] mask back on and get them to a Field Hospital." From the battalion aid station, men moved to the "Ambulance Head," the closest point to the line safely out of reach of German artillery fire. When possible, all gas casualties rode to avoid exertion. Men blinded by chemical agents were usually led to the ambulance head by comrades who could see, although in some instances, large numbers of blinded soldiers groped their way to the rear by holding on to a cord set up by the medics.[38]

When possible, division field hospitals were located in the same general area, with one hospital designated to handle gas victims. At this hospital the division medical officer supervised triage. Soldiers were placed into one of the following categories: fit for duty, immediate return to unit; fit for

Gas casualties from the 2nd Battalion, 326th Infantry, 82nd Division, waiting for evacuation, Argonne Forest, Ardennes, France, 11 October 1918.

Loading 89th Division gas patients at a field hospital north of Royaumeix (St. Mihiel Sector), 8 August 1918, for removal to a base hospital in Toul. Stretcher bearers wear makeshift burlap mittens to protect hands from gas-infected clothing of victims.

duty in twenty-four hours, return to unit; severely gassed, evacuate to an Army hospital. Exhausted men who complained of gas symptoms but who showed no outward signs of having been gassed were held in the division rear for rest, food, and observation. If medics verified their claims to gas poisoning, they too were evacuated.[39]

Division gas hospitals had to be located near a source of water because persistent and even nonpersistent agents clung to clothing, hair, and skin. After admission to a hospital, doughboys stripped off all their clothing and showered. Those casualties with serious symptoms were bathed while still on their stretchers. The bath house of the 2d Division gas hospital had a portable heater and six shower heads. When a doughboy left the showers, medics sprayed his eyes, nose, and throat with bicarbonate of soda. Depending on the diagnosis, the patient might be given a special treatment of alkaline, oxygen, and, if necessary, venesection (bleeding) to counteract the effects of inhaled gas. For those soldiers who had eaten food or drunk water contaminated by gas, doctors prescribed olive or castor oil to coat the irritated stomach linings. When treatment failed to allow free breathing, or when the patient developed additional symptoms, medics immediately evacuated him to a base gas hospital. By November, 1918, the Medical Department was well on its way to developing procedures to handle gas victims.[40]

If American defensive doctrine and procedures for dealing with gas warfare were rudimentary or nonexistent to begin with and evolved during the war, the same was true of offensive gas doctrine and procedures. The American Army's Artillery Corps had not determined its own doctrine for gas warfare prior to entering combat. Instead, U.S. artillerymen borrowed from both the French and British, as well as from the Germans. The first U.S. field manual for the use of chemical artillery shells was a translation of a current French manual. The AEF, emulating the French, classified chemical shell fire into two types of bombardment. The first type, destructive fire, consisted of two minutes of rapid fire with rounds landing in close proximity, so as to create a dense gas cloud that, given surprise, could inflict heavy casualties. The second type, a neutralizing bombardment, was fired over a longer period and was used to lower the enemy's physical resistance and morale. It also interfered with the enemy's activities by forcing him to wear a mask for extended periods of time. Mustard gas best accomplished neutralization according to the AEF field manuals.[41]

AEF manuals identified several kinds of missions that utilized surprise or neutralizing bombardment. For purpose of harassment, a neutralizing fire was used to exhaust and hinder the movement of enemy personnel. Interdiction fire was a kind of neutralizing fire that rendered positions untenable. Barrages in support of an infantry attack were to consist of 25 percent gas, or one gun per battery. The balance of high explosive fire disrupted enemy reinforcements and prevented counterattacks. AEF manuals duplicated German doctrine by ordering the inclusion of gas in all barrages; this would, it was hoped, deceive the enemy into believing a great concentration of gas was being fired at all times and cause him to mask frequently, thus wearing him down physically and mentally and limiting his ability to defend his position.[42]

Artillery counterbattery fire with gas came to be an extremely effective tactic. Before gas shells came into use, the attempt to neutralize enemy batteries on the Western Front required large amounts of high explosive shell. Regardless of the length of time or the number of rounds fired, complete destruction of the enemy's batteries was never accomplished. Between 1914 and 1916 the average length of time required for artillery counterbattery fire to be effective was estimated at over six days. By 1917, gas made it possible to neutralize a known artillery battery in as little as fifteen minutes. Effective counterbattery fire over a wide front could neutralize enemy artillery in only two to four hours. By the spring of 1918, artillery commanders called for gas shells constantly, and the number of rounds fired was limited only by the availability of such shells.[43]

Of special demand was mustard, the agent that had become the king of the chemical war. The effect of mustard shells was so striking that there was a "constant unfilled demand" for them. One division commander remarked that when his cannoneers were at last issued the agent their morale soared. The arrival of mustard from French gas ammunition points in July, 1918, "caused a great jubilee" among AEF division artillerymen. That same month, on 2 July 1918, AEF General Order 107 allowed division gas officers to take an active role in the preparation of all plans involving the extensive use of gas by artillery and special gas troops.[44]

AEF tactical employment of mustard and other chemical agents improved somewhat as artillerymen became more experienced. If, for instance, the exact location of an enemy battery in a wooded area was unknown, an AEF battery would shell the access roads with mustard, rather than waste limited gas shells by dowsing the entire woods. The artillerymen would then fire high explosive shells to damage the access roads and make it difficult for resupply trains trying to reach the battery to avoid contamination. The enemy battery would soon have to move. This tactic was also used to block reinforcements passing through defiles or over bridges. It proved to be an extremely efficient and economical method of counterbattery fire.[45]

Unfortunately, many senior U.S. Army officers remained oblivious to the potential use of chemicals by artillery or special gas troops in the offense. When it came time for the AEF to launch its first major offensives at St. Mihiel and the Meuse-Argonne, the use of gas was minimal. In preparing for the Meuse-Argonne campaign, for example, the U.S. First Army Headquarters studied the spring offensives of 1918, where the Germans literally smothered the Allies with hundreds of thousands of gas shells in a relatively short space of time. To its credit, First Army HQ disseminated this information to its units and, in field orders during the campaign, urged subordinate corps and divisions to use gas. Gas was made available by the French to the Americans in a sufficient quantity to neutralize enemy batteries, strong points, and installations, and to produce casualties. The final decision to utilize gas, however, rested with the corps and division commanders. With little or no doctrine, training, or experience they were reluctant to employ gas. The offensive use of chemical weapons, according to one First Army general, "does not seem to be understood." Army-level operational planning for the campaign included extensive use of gas, but its use by corps and divisions was halting. While the First Army's divisions did gain some confidence in the use of gas towards the end of the campaign, they never really mastered its employment.[46]

After training with the British Special Brigade, the other gas offensive arm of the AEF, the 1st Gas Regiment, went into action on 22 May 1918. The 1st Battalion, 1st Gas Regiment, which consisted of Companies A and B, reported for duty attached to the 26th Division. On 18 June, Company B, temporarily attached to the XXXII French Corps, conducted the regiment's first independent operation. At 2230, seven hundred 8-inch Livens projectors, emplaced the night before and loaded with sixty-pound drums of phosgene, were fired at two targets located 1,500 meters away. The first target was a company of infantry with one *Minenwerfer* (mortar) company and the second a reserve battalion of infantry. Artillery fired shrapnel and high explosive shells in conjunction with the projector attack. A month later prisoners revealed that this attack caused at least fifty casualties, including ten enemy deaths.[47]

The AEF tactical doctrine for the employment of special gas troops cited the advantages of using gas in terms of accuracy, the extended casualty producing area, and lasting results. The doctrine noted the effectiveness of gas for the elimination of well-entrenched targets that high explosive fire could not destroy. The amount and type of chemical agent employed depended on the tactical situation, as well as wind and terrain features. Projectors, the primary weapon of U.S. gas troops, provided "the means for producing casualties and demoralization second to none." When used aggressively, Livens projectors could keep enemy forces off balance; when employed on a quiet front, they could lessen considerably the likelihood of that front being used as a place to rest battle weary troops.[48]

In the offense, special gas troops could be utilized, according to AEF manuals, in five tactical situations. In the first, they would precede an offensive operation, keeping enemy positions in a gas environment until attacking troops arrived. This tactic would cause casualties and demoralize and reduce the "fighting efficiency and morale" of the enemy. Second, gas employed by special troops could eliminate machine gun nests just prior to an attack. AEF 4-inch Stokes mortars offered the best means of eliminating a machine gun position: two to ten Stokes mortars firing phosgene could form a localized concentration, either creating casualties or forcing the masking or the abandonment of the gun. Third, gas was ideal for sustained operations. Each night, gas could be placed on enemy machine gun nests, strongpoints, and troop concentrations, thereby weakening future resistance. Fourth, after friendly forces had taken an objective, reorganized, and consolidated their positions, gas employment acted as a temporary check or block to potential enemy counterattack formations. Fifth, the doctrine stipulated that in a stabilized situation frequent surprise fire with projectors could create the high concentrations of gas on suitable enemy targets from one end of the line to the other needed to harass enemy troops. In addition, local concentrations of gas, fired from Stokes mortars on machine gun nests, mortar positions, strongpoints, trench intersections, and other sensitive points further reduced enemy morale and strength.[49]

In the brief time it was deployed, the 1st Gas Regiment never matched the sophistication of the British Special Brigade. With the return to open warfare, the 1st Gas Regiment made superhuman efforts to meet AEF needs and moved their Stokes mortars with advancing infantry rather than remain in the trenches, as the British did. The regiment mortar men became very proficient in using thermite shells against machine gun positions and in covering advancing infantry with smoke. The regiment did not, however, employ gas during the attack as extensively as it did thermite and smoke. Gas was used, though, in conjunction with smoke, in order to cause enemy troops to expect gas whenever they received smoke. This tactic forced the enemy to mask, further limiting his vision.

Many commanders resisted the employment of special gas troops. The use of gas was new to American commanders, so it came as no surprise to officers of the Gas Regiment that trouble occasionally arose with the unit they were to support. The 1st Gas Regiment company commanders, lieutenants and captains attached to infantry divisions, tried as best they could to explain what results gas would achieve. During the Saint Mihiel operation in the fall of 1918, infantry officers quickly took advantage of the close support furnished by the Gas Regiment, whose mortar crews knocked out German machine gun nests with thermite and created smoke to screen the U.S. infantry. Still, the infantry appeared reluctant to use gas consistently. When the American First Army launched its first attack, the 1st Gas Regiment did not support the offensive with gas.

During the Meuse-Argonne offensive, the 1st Gas Regiment did support American troops with gas. Company E, 1st Gas Regiment, attached to the 28th Infantry Division, bombarded enemy hilltop positions with Stokes mortar rounds of smoke, thermite, and "deceptive gas." Covered by this suppressive fire, doughboys executed a flanking movement and took the hill with very little difficulty. On 2 October 1918, Company F, while in support of the 33d Infantry Division, received authorization to fire fifty-six projectors loaded with phosgene bombs at German units near Bois La Ville. Results of the gas mission were unknown. Soon after, however, German artillery retaliated by firing a number of Yellow Cross rounds at the 33d Infantry Division. As a result, the infantry regiment being supported by the gas company refused to allow it to fire its scheduled second projector attack. The official history of the Gas Regiment indignantly reported that American troops near Bois La Ville constituted a "normal mustard target" for German gunners and that, "irrespective of our gas operations," the locale normally experienced such attacks.[50]

Company F fired one of the largest American gas bombardments of the Meuse-Argonne campaign in support of the French XVII Corps. The men of Company F installed 230 Livens projectors in two nights. To assist in the operation, 100 French soldiers with forty-seven horses pulled narrow-gauge rail cars containing projectors and shells to the front. At exactly 0330 on 16 October 1918, drums of phosgene, fired in a dense fog and rain, fell on a known enemy troop position. Corps artillery fired high explosive shells in conjunction with the attack.[51]

As the Meuse-Argonne operation continued infantry commanders gained confidence in the effectiveness of chemicals and increasingly called upon gas troops to exercise their skills. By the latter stages of the offensive, some division commanders actively sought out gas company commanders to support their operations. The 2d Division staff consulted the supporting gas company in planning an attack and, as a result, projectors were used for the first time preceding a significant American advance. The results confirmed the claims of the gas unit in that a large number of enemy troops became casualties; the gas cloud itself had a demoralizing effect on other German troops as the wind pushed it to the enemy rear.[52]

The initial hesitancy by the AEF to employ gas was judged understandable by an officer of the 1st Gas Regiment. The American Army was unprepared to engage in gas warfare when President Wilson committed it to battle. As a result, the use of chemical weapons and the defense against them became a deadly learning process for all branches of the Army under the stress of battle. Many commanders were simply unwilling to employ a weapon with which they had had no prior experience and which, if used, could invite German retaliation in kind. For those commanders who did allow the use of gas, some became enthusiastic supporters of offensive gas operations; some did not. The American experience with the offensive use of gas remained uneven to the end of the war.[53]

"We Can Never Afford to Neglect the Question"

6

General John J. Pershing, in his *Final Report*, made specific reference to three weapons introduced in World War I and the impact each had on the conduct of the war. The three weapons Pershing listed were the tank, aircraft, and poison gas. Only one, gas, caused him to reflect on its use in any future war. He declared, "Whether or not gas will be employed in future wars is a matter of conjecture, but the effect is so deadly to the unprepared that we can never afford to neglect the question." Pershing, with the experience of the war behind him, pointed out that gas was a significant weapon, but not as a producer of battle deaths.[1]

The AEF suffered 34,249 immediate deaths on the battlefield. Of these, an estimated 200 were caused by gas.* The number of men wounded and evacuated to medical facilities numbered 224,089. Medical Department reports indicate 70,552 of these hospital patients suffered from gas wounds. Of these gas victims, 1,221 died in AEF hospital wards. When looking at the total figures, 27.3 percent of all AEF casualties, dead and wounded, were caused by gas. With respect to the burden gas casualties placed on medical facilities, not to mention the replacement system, a significant 31.4 percent of all AEF wounded were treated in hospitals for gas wounds (Table 2).[2]

Gas in World War I did not have to cause large numbers of casualties to be an effective and versatile weapon. Gas warfare placed additional strain on every aspect of combat. According to British Maj. Gen. Charles H. Foulkes, Commander of the Special Brigade, the "appearance of gas on the battlefield . . . changed the whole *character* of warfare." In World War I, gas was everywhere, in clothing, food, and water. It corroded human skin, internal organs, and even steel weapons. The smell of gas hung in the air, and the chemical environment became a reality of everyday life. Not only did men have to train constantly, but an entire logistical network had to be established for offensive and defensive gas equipment. A new branch of the U.S. Army came into existence, and new units, such as decontamination squads, mobile degassing units, and special gas troops, were created. These organizations, in turn, took manpower away from the combat arms, as

---

*This is a rough and perhaps low estimate. It was always difficult to determine the cause of death when shell-torn bodies were interred by Quartermaster troops.

91

92

combat arms officers became gas officers in divisions, regiments, and battalions. Also, the impact of gas on the Medical Department posed tremendous problems in the treatment of casualties. The number of gas wounded became so great that one field hospital out of four per division was dedicated to the treatment of gas victims.[3]

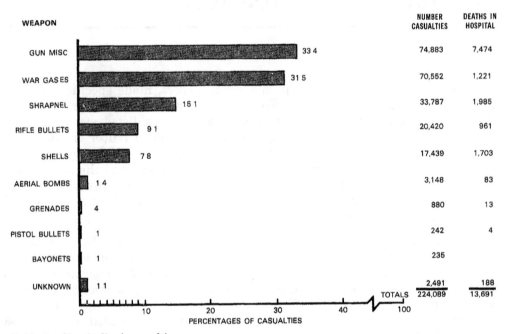

WEAPON		NUMBER CASUALTIES	DEATHS IN HOSPITAL
GUN MISC	33 4	74,883	7,474
WAR GASES	31 5	70,552	1,221
SHRAPNEL	15 1	33,787	1,985
RIFLE BULLETS	9 1	20,420	961
SHELLS	7 8	17,439	1,703
AERIAL BOMBS	1 4	3,148	83
GRENADES	4	880	13
PISTOL BULLETS	1	242	4
BAYONETS	1	235	
UNKNOWN	1 1	2,491	188
TOTALS		224,089	13,691

PERCENTAGES OF CASUALTIES

Table 2. Hospitalized casualties.

Despite the pervasive impact of chemical agents on the battlefield, commanders and staffs had difficulty adjusting their thinking and planning in such a way as to make effective use of these new weapons—weapons totally different from anything they had ever been trained to use. Not only did commanders and staffs have difficulty determining how they would employ the new weapon to their tactical advantage, but they also had to consider the effects of enemy gas on their own troops. By entering the conflict without preparation for chemical warfare, AEF commanders never fully comprehended the potential of gas on the battlefield.

The experience of the United States Army before and during World War I suggests several shortcomings in the military's preparation for, and later employment of, chemical warfare. Prior to American entry into the war, the War Department and General Staff virtually ignored the deployment of chemical weapons in Europe and did little or nothing to prepare the Army to fight and survive in a chemical environment. This pervasive neglect had an adverse impact on the capability of the AEF to fight effectively on a chemical battlefield. American troops entering front-line trenches were usually poorly trained and ill equipped to engage in gas warfare.

Proper defensive equipment is a minimal requirement for the successful engagement of forces in chemical warfare. The indispensable item for the World War I doughboy was his protective mask. Besides the filtration of all harmful agents, the mask had to fulfill a number of other requirements to be efficient. It had to be comfortable and allow for freedom of movement, full vision, easy breathing, communication, and durability. The American failure to develop a mask that could meet these requirements limited the combat effectiveness of the soldiers of the AEF. The decision to purchase the British SBR and, later, to manufacture an American version of it rather than to adopt and modify the more efficient and comfortable French *Tissot* was a serious error in judgment brought about by a lack of foresight and preparation.

The prewar failure to develop and experiment with new gases was also a serious shortcoming. If attention had been paid to the rapidly changing technology of chemical warfare, the United States, with its untapped industrial capacity, might have been able to overcome the German advantage. American technology might have produced the "king" of war gases, the persistent mustard agent, in a timely fashion. Instead, the Germans introduced this agent a year before the Allies.

After entry into the conflict, the United States geared up for production of war gases currently in use. Eventually mustard and other agents were shipped from the United States, but only in fifty-five-gallon containers. Production of chemical shells, based on French designs, was belatedly undertaken, and not a single American gas shell ever left the muzzle of an AEF artillery piece in combat. The unfortunate shortage of gas shells restricted the AEF's capability to retaliate in kind against the Germans; this, in turn, had a demoralizing effect on troops whose own positions had been liberally drenched with gas from German shells.

The AEF never found the key to effective education and training for the offensive and defensive aspects of chemical warfare. A significant advantage could have been obtained if both offensive and defensive training had been integrated into all aspects of instruction. Once a soldier understood the overall nature of gas warfare and acquired confidence in his equipment and gas officers, he more easily accepted and adjusted to chemicals in actual combat. Unfortunately, U.S. training in chemical warfare never reached the sophistication needed to achieve the desired results. Equipment shortages and the lack of trained instructors hampered the AEF's preparation to engage in chemical warfare. The Army suffered needless casualties as a consequence.

Good gas discipline was also essential to the conduct of chemical warfare. Very few soldiers reached the level of the 1st Infantry Division doughboy who, when asked by a staff officer if the gas alarm signified a drill, replied through his mask in muffled tones, "Put on your mask, put on your mask, you damn fool and don't ask questions." "Here," said the division commander who learned of the incident, "was the real thing in discipline." Discipline and training were required if men were to be expected to remain in a contaminated area. The soldier's determination to fight on would certainly have been enhanced if he had had faith in his equipment and the knowledge that provisions had been made for the decontamination of himself and his gear.[4]

Had the U.S. Army's leaders, prior to America's entry into the war, prepared themselves intellectually by studying German gas doctrine or by reviewing observer reports, gas officers would not have had to overcome such strong resistance to the tactical employment of chemicals. Because the U.S. Army failed to develop gas warfare doctrine, the average AEF officer never really understood the potential value of chemicals. Nor could he put aside his preconceived, if perhaps erroneous notion, that chemicals were unusually inhumane weapons whose development should not be pursued. For America the real inhumanity of chemical warfare in World War I lay in the blindness of U.S. civilian and military leaders who, having ignored the real and present threat posed by gas, deployed the doughboys of the AEF to fight unprepared in a chemical environment. Ignorance, short-sightedness, and unpreparedness extracted a high toll at the front, a toll that the United States with its intellectual and technological resources should not have had to pay.

Notes

Introduction

1. Wayne Biddle, "Restocking the Chemical Arsenal," *New York Times Magazine*, 24 May 1981:36.

2. "Poisoning the Battlefield," *Time Magazine*, 10 March 1980:28.

Chapter 1

1. Amos A. Fries and Clarence J. West, *Chemical Warfare* (New York: McGraw-Hill, 1921), 1.

2. Ibid., 2—4; Alden H. Waitt, *Gas Warfare: The Chemical Weapon, Its Use and Protection Against It* (New York: Duell, Sloan, and Pearce, 1942), 7—11.

3. Waitt, *Gas Warfare*, 12—13.

4. Ian V. Hogg, *Gas*, Ballantine's Illustrated History of the Violent Century: Weapons Book no. 43, edited by Barrie Pitt (New York: Ballantine Books, 1975), 10—11; *Army and Navy Journal*, 8 May 1915:1141.

5. Barbara W. Tuchman, *The Guns of August* (New York: MacMillan, 1962), 119.

6. Rudolf Hanslian, *The German Gas Attack at Ypres on April 22, 1915* (Berlin: Verlag Gasschutz and Luftschutz, 1934), 6, translated by the Military Intelligence Division, U.S. Army War College; Charles H. Foulkes, *"Gas!" The Story of the Special Brigade* (Edinburgh: William Blackwood, 1936), 24; Ulrich Müller-Kiel, *Die Chemische Waffe im Weltkrieg und jetzt* [The chemical weapon during the war and now] (Berlin: Verlag Chemie, 1932), 16, translated by the Military Intelligence Division, U.S. Army War College; H. C. Peterson, *Propaganda for War* (Norman: University of Oklahoma Press, 1939), 63; Hogg, *Gas*, 19.

7. Foulkes, *"Gas!"*, 25; Victor Lefebure, *The Riddle of the Rhine: Chemical Strategy in Peace and War* (New York: E. P. Dutton & Co., 1923), 40; Hogg, *Gas*, 20—23; Curt Wachtel, *Chemical Warfare* (Brooklyn, NY: Chemical Publishing Co., 1941), 66.

8. Hogg, *Gas*, 23.

9. Augustin Mitchell Prentiss, *Chemicals in War: A Treatise on Chemical Warfare* (New York: McGraw-Hill Book Co., 1937), 435—36

10. Hanslian, *Ypres*, 6—7; Hogg, *Gas*, 24; Wachtel, *Chemical Warfare*, 64.

11. Hanslian, *Ypres*, 10—12.

12. The description of the first gas attack is taken from the following sources. Hanslian, *Ypres*; Owen Spencer Watkins, unidentified article in *The Methodist Recorder* (Great Britain) quoted in *The Literary Digest*, 4 September 1915:483—86, and Basil Henry Liddell Hart, *The Real War, 1914-1918* (Boston: Little, Brown and Co., 1930), 175—85.

13. Foulkes, *"Gas!"*, 19—20.

14. The description of the British gas attack at Loos is taken from Ibid., 66—84; and Hart, *The Real War*, 186—98.

15. Foulkes, *"Gas!"*, 84.

Chapter 2

1. Müller-Kiel, *Chemische Waffe*, 49.

2. Hogg, *Gas*, 11—14.

3. Rudolf Hanslian, *Der Chemische Krieg* [The chemical war] (Berlin: E.S. Mittler & Sohn, 1927), 64, translated by the U.S Army War College; Foulkes, *"Gas!"*, 263—64

4. Hanslian, *Chemische Krieg*, 4.

5. Great Britain, Army, *Report on the Activities of the Special Brigade*, with chart on "Expansion of the Special Brigade," 19 December 1918, in possession of the author; France, Armée, Armées du Nord et du Nordest, *Instruction relative a l'Organization et a emploi des Unités spéciales, dites, Unités Z* [Instruction relative to the organization and use of special units, called Units Z], 23 January 1918, partial translation by Dr. Robert M. Epstein, Combat Studies Institute, U.S. Army Command and General Staff College, 1982, Hanslian, *Chemische Krieg*, 4. There were thirteen Russian field armies at the time that country left the war.

6. Foulkes, *"Gas!"*, 242—43.

7. Samuel James Manson Auld, "Chemical Warfare," *Chemical Warfare*, 15 March 1922.12—24, reprint of a lecture published in the *Royal Engineers Journal* (Great Britain) of February 1922; Foulkes, *"Gas!"*, 293.

8 Hanslian, *Chemische Krieg*, 4—5; Foulkes, *"Gas!"*, 94—95, 305.

9. Hanslian, *Chemische Krieg*, 48—49.

10. Prentiss, *Chemicals in War*, 440—45.

11. Ibid.

12. Foulkes, *"Gas!"*, 167, 169; Lefebure, *Riddle*, 62.

13. Hanslian, *Chemische Krieg*, 107.

14. Hogg, *Gas*, 48—49; Pascal Lucas, *The Evolution of Tactical Ideas in France and Germany during the War of 1914-1918* (Paris· Berger-Levrault, 1923), 34, translated by P V. Kieffer, U.S. Army, in 1925.

15. Foulkes, *"Gas!"*, 145, 238 n. 145, 191; Donald Wilson, former Major, Special Brigade, Royal Engineers, interview with author, Fort McClellan, AL, 28 October 1981.

16. Foulkes, *"Gas!"*, 197—98.

17 Hanslian, *Chemische Krieg*, 45.

18. Prentiss, *Chemicals*, 458.

19. Hanslian, *Chemische Krieg*, 61.

20. Hogg, *Gas*, 119—20.

21. Hanslian, *Chemische Krieg*, 58.

22. Ibid.

23. Ibid., 63, 67—68; Fries and West, *Chemical Warfare*, 176.

24. Lucas, *Tactical Ideas*, 127.

25. Ibid., 22, Fries and West, *Chemical Warfare*, 205—6.

26. Robert Graves, *Goodbye to All That* (Garden City, NY: Doubleday Anchor Books, 1957, c1929), 95; Prentiss, *Chemicals*, 536.

27. Graves, *Goodbye*, 198.

28. Fries and West, *Chemical Warfare*, 197—98.

29. Prentiss, *Chemicals*, 539.

30. Fries and West, *Chemical Warfare*, 202.

31. Foulkes, *"Gas!"*, 312—13; U.S. War Department, *Gas Warfare*, pt. 1, *German Methods of Offense*, Document no 705 (Washington, DC: U.S. Army War College/U.S. Government Printing Office, 1918), 19, hereafter cited as War Department, *Gas Warfare*, etc.; Prentiss, *Chemicals*, 540.

Chapter 3

1. Frederick Brown, *Chemical Warfare, A Study in Restraints* (Princeton, NJ: Princeton University Press, 1968), 15—17. I confirmed Brown's analysis of the propaganda war by examining prewar issues of the *Army-Navy Journal*, *The Literary Digest*, and the *New York Times*. I also looked at Harold D. Lasswell, *Propaganda in the World War* (New York: Peter Smith, 1938), and Peterson, *Propaganda for War*. Frederick Palmer, an astute wartime observer, gives an excellent overview of the effect Allied propaganda had on Americans in *Newton D. Baker, America at War*, 2 vols. (New York: Dodd, Mead, 1931), 1:36—39 See also Benedict Crowell, *America's Munitions, 1917-1918* (Washington, DC: U.S. Government Printing Office, 1919), 410.

2. Brown, *Chemical Warfare*, 40—41. Brown cites Chief of Staff Peyton C. March's comments that the use of gas "reduces civilization to savagery." From memoirs of World War I officers, especially those who served in the Chemical Warfare Service, it is apparent that this belief was widespread.

3. William A. Ganoe, *The History of the United States Army*, rev. ed. (Ashton, MD: Eric Lundberg, 1964), 452, Brown, *Chemical Warfare*, 21n.

4. U.S. Senate, Committee on Military Affairs, *Preparedness for National Defense*, 64th Cong, 1st sess. (Washington, DC: U.S. Government Printing Office, 1916), 483; Wilder D. Bancroft, et al., *Medical Aspects of Gas Warfare*, The Medical Department of the United States Army in the World War, vol. 14 (Washington, DC: U.S. Government Printing Office, 1926), 27.

5. Bancroft, et al., *Medical Aspects*, 27.

6. Ibid. In *Chemical Warfare*, Brown cites two reports, but these were filed after the U.S declaration of war.

7. U.S. War Department, *Annual Report, 1917*, vol. 1, *The Secretary of War, et al.* (Washington, DC: U.S. Government Printing Office, 1918), 42.

8. Bancroft, et al., *Medical Aspects*, 27.

9. Fries and West, *Chemical Warfare*, 32.

10. Bancroft, et al., *Medical Aspects*, 28.

11. Crowell, *America's Munitions*, 413; G. A. Burrell, "The First Twenty Thousand," *Journal of Industrial Engineering*, 2 (1919), 93, quoted in Fries and West, *Chemical Warfare*, 43.

12. Bancroft, et al., *Medical Aspects*, 28.

13. Ibid.

14. Ibid., 30—31.

15. Ibid., Fries and West, *Chemical Warfare*, 34.

16. Chief, Chemical Warfare Service, to Chief of Staff, A. E. F., 16 October 1918, Subj: Gas Training in [the] United States, reprinted in U.S. Army, Chemical Warfare Service, Defense Division, "Report on the Operations of the Defense Division, Chemical Warfare Service," Submitted to the Chief of Chemical Warfare Service in accordance with S. O. 31, December 1918, DTIC AD-498438, hereafter cited as "Report . . . Defense Division."

17. Edgar Dow Gilman, "Chemical Warfare. Lectures Delivered to the Reserve Officer Training Corps, University of Cincinnati: Gas Projector Attacks," *Chemical Warfare* 8 (15 July 1922):14; Robert Lee Bullard, *Personalities and Reminiscences of the War* (Garden City, NY: Doubleday, Page & Co., 1925), 193.

18. Samuel James Manson Auld, "A General Record of the American Chemical Warfare Service and the Relations Therewith of the British Gas Mission," 5 sect., 2:4, in the author's possession.

19. Ibid., 2:3.

20. Ibid., 1:3—5; Chief, Chemical Warfare Service, A. E. F., to all gas officers, 28 September 1918, Subj: Gas Defense Training, 35th Division Gas Officer File, Record Group 120, National Archives, Washington, DC.

21. Fries and West, *Chemical Warfare*, 66; Division Gas Officer, 29th Division, to Deputy Chief, Chemical Warfare Service, 13 January 1918, uncataloged Division Gas Officer Reports, U.S. Army Military History Institute, Carlisle Barracks, PA, hereafter cited as MHI; Baron Munchausen [pseud], "History of the 318th Field Hospital," World War I project, MHI.

22. Gilman, "Lectures," 16; Memorandum no. 65, HQ, 80th Division, Camp Lee, VA, 14 May 1918, uncataloged Division Gas Officer Reports, MHI.

23. General Order no. 108, 15 August 1917, cited in U.S. Army, A. E. F., 1917-1919, "History of the Chemical Warfare Service, American Expeditionary Forces, First Gas Regiment," 14 pts. in 1 vol. (Bound typescript; Fort Leavenworth, KS: General Service School, n.d.), pt. 1, hereafter cited as A. E. F., "History . . . 1st Gas Regiment"; Ibid., 1:1, 4; Fries and West, *Chemical Warfare*, 42—44.

24. Crowell, *America's Munitions*, 418-28; Lt. Col. Amos A. Fries to Director of the Chemical Warfare Service, 19 March 1919, Subj: "History of Chemical Warfare Service in France," uncataloged manuscript, MHI, 5, 24, 27—29.

25. Crowell, *America's Munitions*, 397; Fries and West, *Chemical Warfare*, 53.

26. E. Alexander Powell, *The Army Behind the Army* (New York: Charles Scribner's Sons, 1919), 125; Crowell, *America's Munitions*, 397—408.

27. Prentiss, *Chemicals*, 81—82.

28. Fries and West, *Chemical Warfare*, 60—70.

Chapter 4

1. U.S. Department of the Army, Historical Division, *United States Army in the World War, 1917-1919*, vol. 16, *General Orders, G. H. Q., A. E. F.*, G. O. no. 8, 5 July 1917, "Organization of Headquarters, American Expeditionary Forces," Table 4, "Technical and Administration Services (Gas Service)" (Washington, DC: U.S. Government Printing Office, 1948), 23, hereafter cited as *General Orders, A. E F*

2. Fries, "History," 2.

3. Ibid.

4. Ibid., 3; *General Orders, A. E F*, G. O no. 31, 3 September 1917, 67—68.

5. *General Orders, A. E. F.*, G. O. no. 79, 27 May 1918, 327—29.

6. Ibid., G. O. no. 107, 2 July 1918, 370.

7. Fries, "History," 5

8. War Department, *Gas Warfare*, pt. 2, *Methods of Defense Against Gas Attacks*, 14—18, Fries, "History," 11, 24, 27; Fries and West, *Chemical Warfare*, 50—51.

9. Fries, "History," 28—29.

10. Ibid., 29.

11. Ibid., 8—9; Crowell, *America's Munitions*, 406—9; Powell, *The Army*, 125, Prentiss, *Chemicals*, 481.

12. Prentiss, *Chemicals*, 462.

13. *General Orders, A. E. F.*, G. O. no 53, 3 November 1917, 100.

14. U.S War Department, *Memorandum on Gas Poisoning in Warfare with Notes on Its Pathology and Treatment* (Washington, DC: U.S Government Printing Office, 1917); Fries, "History," 9—10.

15. U.S. Army, Chemical Warfare Service, Medical Director, "History of Chemical Warfare Service, American Expeditionary Forces, Medical Director" (N.p., 1918), 1, DTIC AD-494989, hereafter cited as "History . . . Medical Director"; Bancroft, et al., *Medical Aspects*, 59

16. "History . . Medical Director," 2—3.

17 Ibid

18. E. W. Spencer, "The History of Gas Attacks upon the American Expeditionary Forces During the World War," 4 pts (Bound typescript; Edgewood Arsenal, MD: Chemical Warfare Service, U.S. War Department, 15 February 1928), 3:403—4; J. W Grissinger, *Medical Field Service in France* (Washington, DC: The Association of Military Surgeons, 1928), 28—29, reprinted from *The Military Surgeon* 61—63 (1927—1928).

19. Grissinger, *Medical Field Service*, 41.

20. *General Orders, A. E. F.*, G. O. no. 144, 29 August 1918, 429—32; Bancroft, et al., *Medical Aspects*, 60, 838.

21. Bancroft, et al., *Medical Aspects*, 45, 49.

22. Fries and West, *Chemical Warfare*, 86; Gilman, "Lectures," 14.

23. Norman A. Dunham, "The War As I Saw It," 3 vols., manuscript, World War I project, MHI, 1:166, 168, Gilman, "Lectures," 14.

24 U.S. Army, Chemical Warfare Service, European Division, "Training Activities of the Chemical Warfare Service" (N.p., 1919) Unless otherwise indicated all of the information pertaining to defensive gas training is from this unnumbered publication

25. "History .   1st Gas Regiment," 1:5—7, 2:9—10.

26. Auld, "General Record," 2:5; U S. Army, A. E. F., 1917-1919, 1st Army, *Provisional Instructions for Artillery Officers on the Use of Gas Shell* (N.p.: Base Printing Plant, 29th Engineers, 1918); U S. Army, A.E.F., 1917-1919, *Gas Manual*, pt. 2, *Use of Gas by the Artillery* (France, March 1919), hereafter cited as *Gas Manual*, pt. 2; U.S. Army, Chemical Warfare Service, "History of the Chemical Warfare Service, American Expeditionary Forces" (N.p , 1918), 43, DTIC AD-495051.

Chapter 5

1 Bullard, *Personalities*, 136.

2. Rexmond C. Cochrane, *The 1st Division at Ansauville, January-April 1918*, U.S. Army Chemical Corps Historical Studies: Gas Warfare in World War I, Study no. 9 (Army Chemical Center, MD: Historical Officer, U.S. Army Chemical Corps, 1958), 12—13.

3. Ibid., 5; U.S. Army, 16th Infantry Regiment, "The Story of the 16th Infantry in France," typescript, World War I project, MHI, 8.

4. War Department, *Gas Warfare*, pt. 3, *Methods of Training in Defensive Measures*, 26—28.

5. Amos A. Fries, -*Gas in Defense*-, in -*Gas in Attack*- and -*Gas in Defense*- (Fort Leavenworth, KS· The General Service Schools Press, n.d.), 17—18, reprinted from the *National Service Magazine*, June-July 1919; "Report . . . Defense Division," 12.

6. "Report . . . Defense Division," 14.

7. Bullard *Personalities*, 159; "Report . . . Defense Division," 14

8. U.S. Army, A. E. F., Office of the Chief of Gas Service, "Semi-monthly Report to Director of Gas Service, U.S., on Activities and Needs of the Gas Service, A. E. F ," 15 May 1918, 2, DTIC AD-498800

9. "Report . . . Defense Division," 14

10. Dorothy Kneeland Clark, *Effectiveness of Chemical Weapons in World War I*, Staff paper ORO-SP-88 (Bethesda, MD: Tactics Division, Operations Research Office, Johns Hopkins University, 1959), 75; U.S. Army, A. E. F., 1917-1919, *Defensive Measures Against Gas Attack*, No. 253 revised (France, November 1917), 8, hereafter cited as *Defensive Measures*.

11. Moses King, "Diary of Moses King, Company I, 305th Infantry, U.S N.A.," n.d., World War I project, MHI; Chief, CWS, to all gas officers, 28 September 1918, RG 120, National Archives.

12. Harry L. Gilchrist, *A Comparative Study of World War Casualties From Gas and Other Weapons* (Edgewood Arsenal, MD: Chemical Warfare School, 1928), 21; "Report . . . Defense Division," 16; Clarence M. Wood, former medic, 140th Ambulance Company, 35th Division, letter to the author, 19 October 1981; Prentiss, *Chemicals in War*, 565.

13. Prentiss, *Chemicals in War*, 564—65; "Report . . . Defense Division"; Fries and West, *Chemical Warfare*, 272—74; Waitt, *Gas Warfare*, 195.

14. *General Orders, A. E. F.*, G. O. no. 144, 29 August 1918, 432; Fries, -*Gas in Defense*-, 15—16.

15. Foulkes, *"Gas!"*, 101—2.

16. Fries -*Gas in Defense*-, 14; War Department, *Gas Warfare*, 2:14.

17. Fries -*Gas in Defense*-, 11; War Department, *Gas Warfare*, 2:31.

18. Rexmond C. Cochrane, *The 42nd Division Before Landres-et-St-Georges, October 1918*, U.S. Army Chemical Corps Historical Studies: Gas Warfare in World War I, Study no. 17 (Army Chemical Center, MD: Historical Office, U.S. Army Chemical Corps, 1960), 13—15.

19. Fries, -Gas in Defense-, 9—10.

20 General Orders, A. E. F., G. O. no. 107, 2 July 1918, 370; Fries and West, Chemical Warfare, 89—91; Charles R. Shrader, Amicicide: The Problem of Friendly Fire in Modern War, Research Survey no. 1 (Fort Leavenworth, KS: Combat Studies Institute, U.S. Army Command and General Staff College, 1982), xii, 2.

21. U.S. Army, 26th Division, Gas Officer, "Report of Growth, Organization and Accomplishments of the Division Gas Officer, With Suggested Duties of Officers," 25 November 1918, Record Group 120, National Archives, Washington, DC.

22. Ibid.

23. Harold Reigelman, "A Chemical Officer at the Front," Chemical Warfare Bulletin 23 (April 1937):42.

24. Ibid., 54.

25. Spencer. "Gas Attacks," pt. 1, "First Division," 8—13.

26. Reigelman, "At the Front," 51.

27. Laurence Stallings, The Doughboys (New York: Harper and Row, 1963), 100—1.

28. Bullard, Personalities, 193.

29. Stallings, The Doughboys, 377; quotation in D. Clayton James, The Years of MacArthur, vol. 1, 1880—1941 (Boston: Houghton Mifflin Co., 1970), 197.

30. Andrew Kachik, "Diary" [of service with the 314th Infantry, 79th Infantry Division], 29 September 1918, World War I project, MHI, George F. Unmacht, "The Effects of Chemical Agents on Quartermaster Supplies," The Quartermaster Review 14 (November-December 1934):54; Fries, -Gas in Defense-, 16; Defensive Measures, 12.

31. Division Gas Officer, 32d Division to Commanding General 32d Division, "Monthly Report," n.d., Record Group 120, National Archives, Washington, DC; Spencer, "Gas Attacks," pt. 1, "1st Division," 3; Regimental Gas Officer, 18th Infantry, to Commanding Officer," 5 May 1918, quoted in Rexmond C. Cochrane, The 1st Division at Cantigny, May 1918, U.S. Army Chemical Corps Historical Studies: Gas Warfare in World War I, Study no. 11 (Army Chemical Center, MD: Historical Office, U.S. Army Chemical Corps, 1958), 19—20; "Report . . . Defense Division," 10, 14; General Orders, A. E. F., G. O. no. 78, 25 May 1918.

32. Clark, Effectiveness, 75; Division Gas Officer, 29th Division, to Chief Gas Officer, 1st Army, "Report on Recent Operations," 20 November 1918, Record Group 120, National Archives, Washington, DC; Willard Newton, "Over There for Uncle Sam: A Daily Diary of World War One," n. d., 95, World War I project, MHI; Division Gas Officer, 29th Division to Chief Gas Officer, 1st Army, A. E. F, "Report on Recent Operations," 20 October 1918, uncataloged Division Gas Officer Files, MHI.

33. Clark, Effectiveness, 73—74.

34. Karl Edwin Harriman, The Cannoneers Have Hairy Ears (New York: J. H. Sear, 1927), 50, 176; Waitt, Gas Warfare, 195.

35. Cochrane, The 42d Division, 9.

36. "History . . . Medical Director," 17; Bancroft, et al., Medical Aspects, 65.

37. "History . . . Medical Director," 17, Bancroft, et al., Medical Aspects, 65.

38. Wood letter.

39. Grissinger, Medical Field Service, 71.

40. Medical Director, Gas Service, to Chief of Gas Service, A. E. F, 1 July 1918, Subj· Report of Second Serious Gas Attack in 2d Division, reprinted in Bancroft, et al., *Medical Aspects*, 71—73.

41. *Gas Manual*, 2:12—13.

42. Ibid., 12.

43. Conrad H. Lanza, "Counterbattery," *Chemical Warfare Bulletin* 23 (July 1937):89—91; Lucas, *Tactical Ideas*, 57.

44. Bullard, *Personalities*, 193—94, General Orders, A E. F., G. O. no. 107, 2 July 1918, 370.

45. Lanza, "Counterbattery," 92.

46. Rexmond C. Cochrane, *The Use of Gas in the Meuse-Argonne Campaign, September-November 1918*, U S. Army Chemical Corps Historical Studies: Gas Warfare in World War I, Study no. 10 (Army Chemical Center, MD: Historical Office, U.S. Army Chemical Corps, 1958), 89; "History . . . 1st Gas Regiment, pt. 3., sect. 6, 1—35; Fries and West, *Chemical Warfare*, 90.

47. "History . . 1st Gas Regiment," 1:1.

48. Ibid., 4:1, 3; pt. 3, sect. 4:8.

49. Ibid., 4 1—2

50. Ibid., 4.3

51. James Thayer Addison, *The Story of the First Gas Regiment* (Boston: Houghton Mifflin Co., 1919), 149—50; "History . . 1st Gas Regiment," pt. 3, sect. 4·8.

52. "History . . . 1st Gas Regiment," pt. 3, sect. 5:14.

53. Addison, *First Gas Regiment*, 150.

Chapter 6

1. John J. Pershing, *Final Report of General John J. Pershing, Commander-in-Chief American Expeditionary Forces* (Washington, DC: U.S. Government Printing Office, 1920), 77.

2. In researching gas casualty statistics, I found minor discrepancies and a variety of reporting methods. The studies I examined included Albert G. Love, *Statistics*, pt. 2, *Medical and Casualty Statistics*, The Medical Department of the United States Army in the World War, vol. 15 (Washington, DC: U.S. Government Printing Office, 1925); Albert G. Love, *War Casualties*, Army Medical Bulletin no. 24 (Carlisle Barracks, PA: Medical Field Service School, 1931); and Harry L. Gilchrist, *A Comparative Study of World War Casualties From Gas and Other Weapons* (Edgewood Arsenal, MD: Chemical Warfare School, 1928). I found that the latter had the clearest format and figures that were substantiated by the other studies. The figures do not include casualties in the Marine Brigade of the 2nd Infantry Division.

3. Foulkes, *"Gas!"*, 345.

4. Bullard. *Personalities*. 161.

Bibliography

Primary Sources

Unpublished

Auld, Samuel James Manson. "A General Record of the American Chemical Warfare Service and the Relations Therewith of the British Gas Mission." 5 sect. In the author's possession.

Chief, Chemical Warfare Service, A. E. F., to all gas officers, 28 September 1918, Subj: Gas Defense Training. 35th Division Gas Officer Files, Record Group 120, National Archives, Washington, DC.

Chief, Chemical Warfare Service, to Chief of Staff, A. E. F., 16 October 1918, Subj: Gas Training in [the] United States. Reprinted in U.S. Army, Chemical Warfare Service, Defense Division, "Report on the Operations of the Defense Division, Chemical Warfare Service." Submitted to the Chief of Chemical Warfare Service in accordance with S. O. 31, December 1918. DTIC AD-498438.

Division Gas Officer, 29th Division, to Chief Gas Officer, 1st Army. "Report on Recent Operations." 20 November 1918. Record Group 120, National Archives, Washington, DC.

Division Gas Officer, 29th Division, to Chief Gas Officer, 1st Army, A. E. F. "Report on Recent Operations." 20 October 1918. Uncataloged Division Gas Officer Files, U.S. Army Military History Institute, Carlisle Barracks, PA.

Division Gas Officer, 29th Division, to Deputy Chief, Chemical Warfare Service, 13 January 1918. Uncataloged Division Gas Officer Reports, U.S. Army Military History Institute, Carlisle Barracks, PA.

Division Gas Officer, 32d Division, to Commanding General, 32d Division. "Monthly Report." N.d. Record Group 120, National Archives, Washington, DC.

Dunham, Norman A. "The War as I Saw It." 3 vols. Manuscript. World War I project, U.S. Army Military History Institute, Carlisle Barracks, PA.

Fries, Amos A., Lt. Col., to Director of the Chemical Warfare Service, 19 March 1919, Subj: "History of Chemical Warfare Service in France." Uncataloged manuscript. U.S. Army Military History Institute, Carlisle Barracks, PA.

Kachik, Andrew. "Diary" [of service with the 314th Regiment, 79th Infantry Division]. World War I project, U.S. Military History Institute, Carlisle Barracks, PA.

King, Moses. "Diary of Moses King, Company I, 305th Infantry, U.S.N.A." N.d. World War I project, U.S. Army Military History Institute, Carlisle Barracks, PA.

Memorandum no. 65, HQ, 80th Division, Camp Lee, VA, 14 May 1918. Uncataloged Division Gas Officer Reports, U.S. Army Military History Institute, Carlisle Barracks, PA.

Munchausen, Baron [pseud.]. "History of the 318th Field Hospital." World War I project, U.S. Army Military History Institute, Carlisle Barracks, PA.

Newton, Willard. "Over There for Uncle Sam: A Daily Diary of World War One." World War I project, U.S. Army Military History Institute, Carlisle Barracks, PA.

Spencer, E. W. "The History of Gas Attacks upon the American Expeditionary Forces During the World War." 4 pts. Bound typescript. Edgewood Arsenal, MD: Chemical Warfare Service, U.S. War Department, 15 February 1928.

U.S. Army. A. E. F., 1917—1919. 1st Gas Regiment. "History of the Chemical Warfare Service, American Expeditionary Forces, 1st Gas Regiment." 14 pts. in 1 vol. Bound typescript. Fort Leavenworth, KS: General Service School, n.d.

_____. Office of the Chief of Gas Service. "Semi-monthly Report to Director of Gas Service, U.S., on Activities and Needs of the Gas Service, A. E. F." 15 May 1918. DTIC AD-498800.

U.S. Army. Chemical Warfare Service. "History of the Chemical Warfare Service, American Expeditionary Forces." N.p., 1918.

_____. Defense Division. "Report on the Operations of the Defense Division, Chemical Warfare Service." Submitted to the Chief of Chemical Warfare Service in accordance with S. O. 31, December 1918. DTIC AD-498438.

_____. European Division. "Training Activities of the Chemical Warfare Service." N.p., 1919.

_____. Medical Director. "History of Chemical Warfare Service, American Expeditionary Forces, Medical Director." N.p., 1918. DTIC AD-494989.

U.S. Army. 26th Division. Gas Officer. "Report of Growth, Organization and Accomplishments of the Division Gas Office, with Suggested Duties of Officers." 25 November 1918. Record Group 120, National Archives, Washington, DC.

U.S. Army. 16th Infantry Regiment. "The Story of the 16th Infantry in France." Typescript. World War I project, U.S. Army Military History Institute, Carlisle Barracks, PA.

Wilson, Donald, former Major, Special Brigade, Royal Engineers. Interview with author. Fort McClellan, AL, 28 October 1981.

Wood, Clarence M., former medic, 140th Ambulance Co., 35th Division. Letter to author. 19 October 1981. In the author's possession.

Published

Addison, James Thayer. *The Story of the First Gas Regiment*. Boston: Houghton Mifflin Co., 1919.

Army and Navy Journal, 8 May 1915:1141.

Auld, Samuel James Manson. "Chemical Warfare." *Chemical Warfare*, 15 March 1922:12—24. Reprint of a lecture published in the *Royal Engineers Journal* (Great Britain) of February 1922.

Bullard, Robert Lee. *Personalities and Reminiscences of the War*. Garden City, NY: Doubleday, Page & Co., 1925.

Burrell, G. A. "The First Twenty Thousand." *Journal of Industrial Engineering* 2 (1919). Quotation in Amos A. Fries and Clarence J. West, *Chemical Warfare*. New York: McGraw-Hill, 1921.

Crowell, Benedict. *America's Munitions, 1917—1918*. Washington, DC: U.S. Government Printing Office, 1919.

Foulkes, Charles H. *"Gas!" The Story of the Special Brigade*. Edinburgh: William Blackwood, 1936.

France. Armée. Armées du Nord et du Nordest. *Instruction relative a l'Organization et a emploi des Unités spéciales, dites, Unités Z* [Instruction relative to the organization and use of special units, called Units Z]. 23 January 1918. Partial translation by Dr. Robert M. Epstein, Combat Studies Institute, U.S. Army Command and General Staff College, 1982.

Fries, Amos A. -Gas in Defense-. In -Gas in Attack- and -Gas in Defense-. Fort Leavenworth, KS?: The General Service Schools, n.d.? Reprinted from the *National Service Magazine*, June-July 1919.

Fries, Amos A., and Clarence J. West. *Chemical Warfare*. New York: McGraw-Hill, 1921.

Gilman, Edgar Dow. "Chemical Warfare. Lectures Delivered to the Reserve Officer Training Corps, University of Cincinnati: Gas Projector Attacks." *Chemical Warfare* 8 (15 July 1922):11—16.

Graves, Robert. *Goodbye to All That*. Garden City, NY: Doubleday Anchor Books. 1957. c1929.

Great Britain. Army. *Report on the Activities of the Special Brigade.* With chart on "Expansion of the Special Brigade." 19 December 1918. In the author's possession.

Grissinger, J. W. *Medical Field Service in France.* Washington, DC: The Association of Military Surgeons, 1928.

Harriman, Karl Edwin. *The Cannoneers Have Hairy Ears.* New York: J. H. Sear, 1927.

Lucas, Pascal. *The Evolution of Tactical Ideas in France and Germany During the War of 1914—1918.* Paris: Berger-Levrault, 1923. Translated by P. V. Kieffer, U.S. Army, in 1925.

Pershing, John J. *Final Report of General John J. Pershing, Commander-in-Chief American Expeditionary Forces.* Washington, DC: U.S. Government Printing Office, 1920.

Reigelman, Harold. "A Chemical Officer at the Front." *Chemical Warfare Bulletin* 23 (April, July, and October 1937):42—55, 106—16, 151—63. Reprinted from *War Notes of a Casual,* publication information unknown.

U.S. Army. A. E. F., 1917—1919. *Defensive Measures Against Gas Attack.* No. 253, revised. France, November 1917.

_____. Gas Manual. Pt. 2. *Use of Gas by the Artillery.* France, March 1919.

_____. 1st Army. *Provisional Instructions for Artillery Officers on the Use of Gas Shell.* N.p.: Base Printing Plant, 29th Engineers, 1918.

U.S. Department of the Army. Historical Division. *United States Army in the World War, 1917—1919.* Vol. 16. *General Orders, G. H. Q., A. E. F.* Washington, DC: U.S. Government Printing Office, 1948.

U.S. Senate. Committee on Military Affairs. *Preparedness for National Defense.* 64th Cong., 1st sess. Washington, DC: U.S. Government Printing Office, 1916.

U.S. War Department. *Annual Report, 1917.* Vol. 1. *The Secretary of War, et al.* Washington, DC: U.S. Government Printing Office, 1918.

_____. *Gas Warfare.* Pt. 1. *German Methods of Offense.* Pt. 2. *Methods of Defense Against Gas Attacks.* Pt. 3. *Methods of Training in Defensive Measures.* Washington, DC: U.S. Army War College/U.S. Government Printing Office, 1918.

_____. *Memorandum on Gas Poisoning in Warfare with Notes on Its Pathology and Treatment.* Washington, DC: U.S. Government Printing Office, 1917.

Watkins, Owen Spencer. Unidentified article in *The Methodist Recorder* (Great Britain) quoted in *The Literary Digest,* 4 September 1915:483—86.

Other Works

Bancroft, Wilder D., et al. *Medical Aspects of Gas Warfare.* The Medical Department of the United States Army in the World War, vol. 14. Washington, DC: U.S. Government Printing Office, 1926.

Biddle, Wayne. "Restocking the Chemical Arsenal." *New York Times Magazine,* 24 May 1981.

Brown, Frederick. *Chemical Warfare, a Study in Restraints.* Princeton, NJ: Princeton University Press, 1968.

Clark, Dorothy Kneeland. *Effectiveness of Chemical Weapons in World War I.* Staff paper ORO-SP-88. Bethesda, MD: Tactics Division, Operations Research Office, Johns Hopkins University, 1959. DTIC AD-233081.

Cochrane, Rexmond C. *The 1st Division at Ansauville, January-April 1918.* U.S. Army Chemical Corps Historical Studies: Gas Warfare in World War I, Study no. 9. Army Chemical Center, MD: Historical Office, U.S. Army Chemical Corps, 1958.

_____. *The 1st Division at Cantigny, May 1918.* U.S. Army Chemical Corps Historical Studies: Gas Warfare in World War I, Study no. 11. Army Chemical Center, MD: Historical Office, U.S. Army Chemical Corps, 1958.

_____. *The 42nd Division Before Landres-et-St. Georges, October 1918.* U.S. Army Chemical Corps Historical Studies: Gas Warfare in World War I, Study no. 17. Army Chemical Center, MD: Historical Office, U.S. Army Chemical Corps, 1960.

_____. *The Use of Gas in the Meuse-Argonne Campaign, September-November 1918.* U.S. Army Chemical Corps Historical Studies: Gas Warfare in World War I, Study no. 10. Army Chemical Center, MD: Historical Office, U.S. Army Chemical Corps, 1958.

Ganoe, William A. *The History of the United States Army.* Rev. ed. Ashton, MD: Eric Lundberg, 1964.

Gilchrist, Harry L., Col. *A Comparative Study of World War Casualties from Gas and Other Weapons.* Edgewood Arsenal, MD: Chemical Warfare School, 1928.

Hanslian, Rudolf. *Der Chemische Krieg* [The chemical war]. Berlin: E. S. Mittler & Sohn, 1927. Translated by the U.S. Army War College.

_____. *The German Gas Attack at Ypres on April 22, 1915.* Berlin: Verlag Gasschutz and Luftschutz, 1934. Translated by the Military Intelligence Division, U.S. Army War College.

Hogg, Ian V. *Gas.* Ballantine's Illustrated History of the Violent Century: Weapons Book no. 43, edited by Barrie Pitt. New York: Ballantine Books, 1975.

James, D. Clayton. *The Years of MacArthur.* Vol. 1. *1880–1941.* Boston: Houghton Mifflin Co., 1970.

Lanza, Conrad H. "Counterbattery." *Chemical Warfare Bulletin* 23 (July 1937):87—94.

Lasswell, Harold D. *Propaganda in the World War*. New York: Peter Smith, 1938.

Lefebure, Victor. *The Riddle of the Rhine: Chemical Strategy in Peace and War*. New York: E. P. Dutton & Co., 1923.

Liddell Hart, Basil Henry. *The Real War, 1914—1918*. Boston: Little, Brown and Co., 1930.

Love, Albert G., Maj. *Statistics*. Pt. 2. *Medical and Casualty Statistics*. The Medical Department of the United States Army in the World War, vol. 15. Washington, DC: U.S. Government Printing Office, 1925.

————. *War Casualties*. Army Medical Bulletin no. 24. Carlisle Barracks, PA: Medical Field Service School, 1931.

Müller-Kiel, Ulrich. *Die Chemische Waffe im Weltkrieg und Jetzt* [The chemical weapon in the World War and now]. Berlin: Verlag Chemie, 1932. Translated by the Military Intelligence Division, U.S. Army War College.

Palmer, Frederick. *Newton D. Baker, America at War*. 2 vols. New York: Dodd, Mead, 1931.

Peterson, H. C. *Propaganda for War*. Norman: University of Oklahoma Press, 1939.

"Poisoning the Battlefield." *Time Magazine*, 10 March 1980:28.

Powell, E. Alexander. *The Army Behind the Army*. New York: Charles Scribner's Sons, 1919.

Prentiss, Augustin Mitchell. *Chemicals in War: A Treatise on Chemical Warfare*. New York: McGraw-Hill Book Co., 1937.

Shrader, Charles R. *Amicicide: The Problem of Friendly Fire in Modern War*. Research Survey no. 1. Fort Leavenworth, KS: Combat Studies Institute, U.S. Army Command and General Staff College, 1982.

Stallings, Laurence. *The Doughboys*. New York: Harper and Row, 1963.

Tuchman, Barbara W. *The Guns of August*. New York: Macmillan, 1962.

Unmacht, George F. "The Effects of Chemical Agents on Quartermaster Supplies." *The Quartermaster Review* 14 (November-December 1934):53—55.

Wachtel, Curt. *Chemical Warfare*. Brooklyn, NY: Chemical Publishing Co., 1941.

Waitt, Alden H. *Gas Warfare: The Chemical Weapon, Its Use and Protection Against It*. New York: Duell, Sloan and Pearce, 1942.

Major(P) Charles E. Heller, USAR, is currently on an AGR tour at the U.S. Army Command and General Staff College as the Combat Studies Institute's USAR Staff Officer. He has served on active duty with the 8th Infantry Division and in a variety of USAR assignments, including a MOBDES position with the U.S. Army Center of Military History. He has an M.A. in history from the University of Massachusetts and has recently completed all his degree requirements for a Ph.D. at the same institution. He has published a number of articles on a variety of military history topics.

Printed in the USA
CPSIA information can be obtained
at www.ICGtesting.com
LVHW080630281123
765119LV00011B/670